MIKHAIL GORBACHEV

MIKHAIL GORBACHEV

Thomas Butson

CHELSEA HOUSE PUBLISHERS
NEW YORK
PHILADELPHIA

SENIOR EDITOR: William P. Hansen
PROJECT EDITOR: John W. Selfridge
ASSOCIATE EDITOR: Marian W. Taylor
EDITORIAL COORDINATOR: Karyn Gullen Browne
EDITORIAL STAFF: Maria Behan
Perry Scott King
Kathleen McDermott
Howard Ratner
Alma Rodriguez-Sokol
LAYOUT: Irene Friedman
ART ASSISTANTS: Noreen Lamb
Carol McDougall
Victoria Tomaselli
COVER ILLUSTRATION: Robin Peterson
PICTURE RESEARCH: Brian Araujo

Frontispiece courtesy of Canapress

7 9 8

Library of Congress Cataloging in Publication Data

Butson, Thomas G. MIKHAIL GORBACHEV.

(World leaders past & present)
Bibliography: p.
Includes index.
  1. Gorbachev, Mikhail Sergeevich, 1931–   . 2. Heads of
state—Soviet Union—Biography. I. Title. II. Series.
DK290.3.G67B875   1986   947.085'4 [92] 86-13706

ISBN 1-55546-200-6
   0-7910-0571-2 (pbk.)

Contents

John Adams
John Quincy Adams
Konrad Adenauer
Alexander the Great
Salvador Allende
Marc Antony
Corazon Aquino
Yasir Arafat
King Arthur
Hafez al-Assad
Kemal Atatürk
Attila
Clement Attlee
Augustus Caesar
Menachem Begin
David Ben-Gurion
Otto von Bismarck
Léon Blum
Simon Bolívar
Cesare Borgia
Willy Brandt
Leonid Brezhnev
Julius Caesar
John Calvin
Jimmy Carter
Fidel Castro
Catherine the Great
Charlemagne
Chiang Kai-Shek
Winston Churchill
Georges Clemenceau
Cleopatra
Constantine the Great
Hernán Cortés
Oliver Cromwell
Georges-Jacques
  Danton
Jefferson Davis
Moshe Dayan
Charles de Gaulle
Eamon De Valera
Eugene Debs
Deng Xiaoping
Benjamin Disraeli
Alexander Dubček
François & Jean-Claude
  Duvalier
Dwight Eisenhower
Eleanor of Aquitaine
Elizabeth I
Faisal
Ferdinand & Isabella
Francisco Franco
Benjamin Franklin

Frederick the Great
Indira Gandhi
Mohandas Gandhi
Giuseppe Garibaldi
Amin & Bashir Gemayel
Genghis Khan
William Gladstone
Mikhail Gorbachev
Ulysses S. Grant
Ernesto "Che" Guevara
Tenzin Gyatso
Alexander Hamilton
Dag Hammarskjöld
Henry VIII
Henry of Navarre
Paul von Hindenburg
Hirohito
Adolf Hitler
Ho Chi Minh
King Hussein
Ivan the Terrible
Andrew Jackson
James I
Wojciech Jaruzelski
Thomas Jefferson
Joan of Arc
Pope John XXIII
Pope John Paul II
Lyndon Johnson
Benito Juárez
John Kennedy
Robert Kennedy
Jomo Kenyatta
Ayatollah Khomeini
Nikita Khrushchev
Kim Il Sung
Martin Luther King, Jr.
Henry Kissinger
Kublai Khan
Lafayette
Robert E. Lee
Vladimir Lenin
Abraham Lincoln
David Lloyd George
Louis XIV
Martin Luther
Judas Maccabeus
James Madison
Nelson & Winnie
  Mandela
Mao Zedong
Ferdinand Marcos
George Marshall

Mary, Queen of Scots
Tomáš Masaryk
Golda Meir
Klemens von Metternich
James Monroe
Hosni Mubarak
Robert Mugabe
Benito Mussolini
Napoléon Bonaparte
Gamal Abdel Nasser
Jawaharlal Nehru
Nero
Nicholas II
Richard Nixon
Kwame Nkrumah
Daniel Ortega
Mohammed Reza Pahlavi
Thomas Paine
Charles Stewart
  Parnell
Pericles
Juan Perón
Peter the Great
Pol Pot
Muammar el-Qaddafi
Ronald Reagan
Cardinal Richelieu
Maximilien Robespierre
Eleanor Roosevelt
Franklin Roosevelt
Theodore Roosevelt
Anwar Sadat
Haile Selassie
Prince Sihanouk
Jan Smuts
Joseph Stalin
Sukarno
Sun Yat-sen
Tamerlane
Mother Teresa
Margaret Thatcher
Josip Broz Tito
Toussaint L'Ouverture
Leon Trotsky
Pierre Trudeau
Harry Truman
Queen Victoria
Lech Walesa
George Washington
Chaim Weizmann
Woodrow Wilson
Xerxes
Emiliano Zapata
Zhou Enlai

CHELSEA HOUSE PUBLISHERS

ON LEADERSHIP

Arthur M. Schlesinger, jr.

LEADERSHIP, it may be said, is really what makes the world go round. Love no doubt smooths the passage; but love is a private transaction between consenting adults. Leadership is a public transaction with history. The idea of leadership affirms the capacity of individuals to move, inspire, and mobilize masses of people so that they act together in pursuit of an end. Sometimes leadership serves good purposes, sometimes bad; but whether the end is benign or evil, great leaders are those men and women who leave their personal stamp on history.

Now, the very concept of leadership implies the proposition that individuals can make a difference. This proposition has never been universally accepted. From classical times to the present day, eminent thinkers have regarded individuals as no more than the agents and pawns of larger forces, whether the gods and goddesses of the ancient world or, in the modern era, race, class, nation, the dialectic, the will of the people, the spirit of the times, history itself. Against such forces, the individual dwindles into insignificance.

So contends the thesis of historical determinism. Tolstoy's great novel *War and Peace* offers a famous statement of the case. Why, Tolstoy asked, did millions of men in the Napoleonic Wars, denying their human feelings and their common sense, move back and forth across Europe slaughtering their fellows? "The war," Tolstoy answered, "was bound to happen simply because it was bound to happen." All prior history predetermined it. As for leaders, they, Tolstoy said, "are but the labels that serve to give a name to an end and, like labels, they have the least possible connection with the event." The greater the leader, "the more conspicuous the inevitability and the predestination of every act he commits." The leader, said Tolstoy, is "the slave of history."

Determinism takes many forms. Marxism is the determinism of class. Nazism the determinism of race. But the idea of men and women as the slaves of history runs athwart the deepest human instincts. Rigid determinism abolishes the idea of human freedom—

the assumption of free choice that underlies every move we make, every word we speak, every thought we think. It abolishes the idea of human responsibility, since it is manifestly unfair to reward or punish people for actions that are by definition beyond their control. No one can live consistently by any deterministic creed. The Marxist states prove this themselves by their extreme susceptibility to the cult of leadership.

More than that, history refutes the idea that individuals make no difference. In December 1931 a British politician crossing Park Avenue in New York City between 76th and 77th Streets around 10:30 P.M. looked in the wrong direction and was knocked down by an automobile—a moment, he later recalled, of a man aghast, a world aglare: "I do not understand why I was not broken like an eggshell or squashed like a gooseberry." Fourteen months later an American politician, sitting in an open car in Miami, Florida, was fired on by an assassin; the man beside him was hit. Those who believe that individuals make no difference to history might well ponder whether the next two decades would have been the same had Mario Constasino's car killed Winston Churchill in 1931 and Giuseppe Zangara's bullet killed Franklin Roosevelt in 1933. Suppose, in addition, that Adolf Hitler had been killed in the street fighting during the Munich *Putsch* of 1923 and that Lenin had died of typhus during World War I. What would the 20th century be like now?

For better or for worse, individuals do make a difference. "The notion that a people can run itself and its affairs anonymously," wrote the philosopher William James, "is now well known to be the silliest of absurdities. Mankind does nothing save through initiatives on the part of inventors, great or small, and imitation by the rest of us—these are the sole factors in human progress. Individuals of genius show the way, and set the patterns, which common people then adopt and follow."

Leadership, James suggests, means leadership in thought as well as in action. In the long run, leaders in thought may well make the greater difference to the world. But, as Woodrow Wilson once said, "Those only are leaders of men, in the general eye, who lead in action. . . . It is at their hands that new thought gets its translation into the crude language of deeds." Leaders in thought often invent in solitude and obscurity, leaving to later generations the tasks of imitation. Leaders in action—the leaders portrayed in this series—have to be effective in their own time.

And they cannot be effective by themselves. They must act in response to the rhythms of their age. Their genius must be adapted, in a phrase of William James's, "to the receptivities of the moment." Leaders are useless without followers. "There goes the mob," said the French politician hearing a clamor in the streets. "I am their leader. I must follow them." Great leaders turn the inchoate emotions of the mob to purposes of their own. They seize on the opportunities of their time, the hopes, fears, frustrations, crises, potentialities. They succeed when events have prepared the way for them, when the community is awaiting to be aroused, when they can provide the clarifying and organizing ideas. Leadership ignites the circuit between the individual and the mass and thereby alters history.

It may alter history for better or for worse. Leaders have been responsible for the most extravagant follies and most monstrous crimes that have beset suffering humanity. They have also been vital in such gains as humanity has made in individual freedom, religious and racial tolerance, social justice, and respect for human rights.

There is no sure way to tell in advance who is going to lead for good and who for evil. But a glance at the gallery of men and women in *World Leaders—Past and Present* suggests some useful tests.

One test is this: Do leaders lead by force or by persuasion? By command or by consent? Through most of history leadership was exercised by the divine right of authority. The duty of followers was to defer and to obey. "Theirs not to reason why / Theirs but to do and die." On occasion, as with the so-called enlightened despots of the 18th century in Europe, absolutist leadership was animated by humane purposes. More often, absolutism nourished the passion for domination, land, gold, and conquest and resulted in tyranny.

The great revolution of modern times has been the revolution of equality. The idea that all people should be equal in their legal condition has undermined the old structure of authority, hierarchy, and deference. The revolution of equality has had two contrary effects on the nature of leadership. For equality, as Alexis de Tocqueville pointed out in his great study *Democracy in America*, might mean equality in servitude as well as equality in freedom.

"I know of only two methods of establishing equality in the political world," Tocqueville wrote. "Rights must be given to every citizen, or none at all to anyone . . . save one, who is the master of all." There was no middle ground "between the sovereignty of all and the absolute power of one man." In his astonishing prediction of 20th-century totalitarian dictatorship, Tocqueville explained how the revolution of equality could lead to the *"Führerprinzip"* and more terrible absolutism than the world had ever known.

But when rights are given to every citizen and the sovereignty of all is established, the problem of leadership takes a new form, becomes more exacting than ever before. It is easy to issue commands and enforce them by the rope and the stake, the concentration camp and the *gulag*. It is much harder to use argument and achievement to overcome opposition and win consent. The Founding Fathers of the United States understood the difficulty. They believed that history had given them the opportunity to decide, as Alexander Hamilton wrote in the first Federalist Paper, whether men are indeed capable of basing government on "reflection and choice, or whether they are forever destined to depend . . . on accident and force."

Government by reflection and choice called for a new style of leadership and a new quality of followership. It required leaders to be responsive to popular concerns, and it required followers to be active and informed participants in the process. Democracy does not eliminate emotion from politics; sometimes it fosters demagoguery; but it is confident that, as the greatest of democratic leaders put it, you cannot fool all of the people all of the time. It measures leadership by results and retires those who overreach or falter or fail.

It is true that in the long run despots are measured by results too. But they can postpone the day of judgment, sometimes indefinitely, and in the meantime they can do infinite harm. It is also true that democracy is no guarantee of virtue and intelligence in government, for the voice of the people is not necessarily the voice of God. But democracy, by assuring the right of opposition, offers built-in resistance to the evils inherent in absolutism. As the theologian Reinhold Niebuhr summed it up, "Man's capacity for justice makes democracy possible, but man's inclination to injustice makes democracy necessary."

A second test for leadership is the end for which power is sought. When leaders have as their goal the supremacy of a master race or the promotion of totalitarian revolution or the acquisition and exploitation of colonies or the protection of greed and privilege or the preservation of personal power, it is likely that their leadership will do little to advance the cause of humanity. When their goal is the abolition of slavery, the liberation of women, the enlargement of opportunity for the poor and powerless, the extension of equal rights to racial minorities, the defense of the freedoms of expression and opposition, it is likely that their leadership will increase the sum of human liberty and welfare.

Leaders have done great harm to the world. They have also conferred great benefits. You will find both sorts in this series. Even "good" leaders must be regarded with a certain wariness. Leaders are not demigods; they put on their trousers one leg after another just like ordinary mortals. No leader is infallible, and every leader needs to be reminded of this at regular intervals. Irreverence irritates leaders but is their salvation. Unquestioning submission corrupts leaders and demeans followers. Making a cult of a leader is always a mistake. Fortunately hero worship generates its own antidote. "Every hero," said Emerson, "becomes a bore at last."

The signal benefit the great leaders confer is to embolden the rest of us to live according to our own best selves, to be active, insistent, and resolute in affirming our own sense of things. For great leaders attest to the reality of human freedom against the supposed inevitabilities of history. And they attest to the wisdom and power that may lie within the most unlikely of us, which is why Abraham Lincoln remains the supreme example of great leadership. A great leader, said Emerson, exhibits new possibilities to all humanity. "We feed on genius. . . . Great men exist that there may be greater men."

Great leaders, in short, justify themselves by emancipating and empowering their followers. So humanity struggles to master its destiny, remembering with Alexis de Tocqueville: "It is true that around every man a fatal circle is traced beyond which he cannot pass; but within the wide verge of that circle he is powerful and free; as it is with man, so with communities."

1

The Soviet Union's Leading Man

On March 11, 1985, the winds of change began to blow through the long-quiet corridors of Moscow's Kremlin, the administrative and political center of the Union of Soviet Socialist Republics (USSR). The Central Committee of the Communist party of the Soviet Union (CPSU) met to elect a new general secretary to succeed the former incumbent, Konstantin Chernenko, who had died the previous day, at age 73. The man they chose was 54-year-old Mikhail Gorbachev. Now, for the first time in three decades the Soviet Union, whose aged leaders had come to be referred to by Western commentators as a "gerontocracy," had an energetic, younger man at the helm.

Many people — ordinary Soviet citizens, government officials, and Western observers alike — had expected that Chernenko's successor would be as elderly (and, in all probability, just as infirm) as Chernenko had been at the time of his own election, in February 1984. During the three decades prior to Chernenko's death, the Soviets had become increasingly accustomed to being ruled by elder statesmen. Between 1964 and 1980, the average age

After years of halting rule by feeble old men, the Soviet Union suddenly has a leader who looks like he belongs at the helm.
—*Newsweek*, March 25, 1985

In December 1984, four months before he was appointed general secretary of the Communist party of the Soviet Union (CPSU), Mikhail Sergeevich Gorbachev traveled to Great Britain at the head of a delegation of Soviet parliamentarians. Here, Gorbachev, followed by two of his colleagues, arrives at London's Heathrow Airport.

TASS FROM SOVFOTO

Accompanied by their aides, Gorbachev and Indian Prime Minister Rajiv Gandhi (at right) walk through the grounds of Moscow's Kremlin — the administrative and political center of the USSR — in May 1985. The cultivation of good relations with India has been a major priority of Soviet foreign policy ever since that country gained its independence from Great Britain in 1947.

of the CPSU's Central Committee secretaries, *Politburo* (political bureau) members, and Politburo candidate (or nonvoting) members had risen from 55.9 to 66, reflecting the reluctance of the older generation of Soviet leaders to allow their younger colleagues to take the reins of power. Gorbachev's election suggested the beginning of a new era in Soviet politics.

Scarcely a month after the election, the scale of the break with the past represented by Gorbachev's accession became even more apparent. The new general secretary did something that Soviet leaders have rarely shown any inclination to do in the 68 years that have elapsed since the founding of the Soviet state: he left the Kremlin to meet the people. Scenes from Gorbachev's tour of Moscow (which included visits to a truck factory, a hospital, a school, and the apartment of an "ordinary" young couple) were broadcast on Soviet television later that day, and transcripts of his conversations appeared on the front pages of *Pravda* and *Izvestia*, the two most prominent Soviet newspapers.

Gorbachev's vigor, informality, and eagerness to talk made him seem more like a Western politician campaigning for public support than a Soviet bureaucrat. His demeanor showed no trace of the reticence and reserve that often characterize senior Soviet officials on public occasions. Gorbachev proved that, unlike several of his predecessors and the majority of his colleagues, he was not afraid to go out into the streets in person to meet the people. One office worker said: "It's about time we had someone like this, who wants to talk with us."

When Gorbachev made an official visit to Leningrad — the second largest city in the Soviet Union — in May 1985, he hit the streets once again, drawing crowds even more enthusiastic than those in Moscow. Soviet television showed a grinning and confident Gorbachev joking with the crowds and fielding questions. At one point, he asked the Leningraders for their advice. "Just get close to the people and we'll not let you down," one woman shouted. "Can I be any closer?" Gorbachev replied with a grin. The elated crowd guffawed with delight.

In just a few months, Gorbachev proved himself a master of Western-style public relations, and became, for a while, a darling of the media both at home and abroad. Accustomed to the prepared speeches of stony-faced, frail old men, Soviets and foreigners alike welcomed Gorbachev's youth, charm, and spontaneity. The Western media gave so much coverage to the charismatic general secretary that one official complained, "Gorbachev's getting more camera time than Brooke Shields."

Just how different is the new general secretary? The Soviet Union has not been governed by such a well-educated and well-traveled man since the days of Vladimir Ilich Lenin, the architect of the Russian Revolution of 1917 and ruler of the Soviet state from 1917 until his death in 1924. Gorbachev is the first Soviet leader, after Lenin, to hold a law degree, and the first ever to hold a degree in agronomy (the science of agricultural management). None of Gorbachev's predecessors had more than a rudimentary education. Joseph Stalin, who ruled the country with an iron fist from 1924 until his death in 1953, received his only formal education at Russian Orthodox schools and seminaries in his native Geor-

He is not a revolutionary. He did not reach the pinnacle by upsetting bureaucratic applecarts or preaching heresies. He won't change the basic system.
—ED A. HEWETT
American expert on Soviet affairs, the Brookings Institution

Gorbachev meets with Soviet citizens in Kiev, the capital of the Ukraine, on June 25, 1985. Unlike several of his predecessors and the majority of his colleagues, Gorbachev regularly takes the opportunity to go out into the streets in person to meet the people.

TASS FROM SOVFOTO

gia, a province in southern Russia. Stalin did not even write in Russian, the official language of the Soviet Union, until he was 20 years old.

Gorbachev is also much different than the majority of his predecessors in that he has far more experience of the world beyond his country's borders than any Soviet leader since Lenin. Indeed, in this context the contrast between Gorbachev and his predecessors is stunning. Stalin spent a total of less than four months outside Russia, all before 1913. Nikita Khrushchev, who was first (general) secretary of the CPSU from 1953 to 1964, attended United Nations meetings in New York in 1959 and 1960. Gorbachev, however, has frequently traveled abroad — unusual for a Soviet official who is not a member of the diplomatic service. He has visited many Eastern and Western European countries, as well as Mongolia, Vietnam, Great Britain, and Canada.

In the course of his visits to the West, Gorbachev has taken a great interest in Western agricultural and industrial management techniques. In both Canada and Great Britain, he asked to be shown around farms and factories so that he could see for himself how they were run. During such tours, he demonstrated the practical side of his nature, questioning the workers on a variety of job-related topics, including wages, benefits, and incentives.

Gorbachev is, above all, the herald of a new generation of Soviet leaders. He and his peers were born after the Russian Revolution; they were too young to fight during the four years of war that followed the German invasion of their homeland in 1941; and they grew to maturity at a time when the brutal repression that had characterized Stalin's rule during the 1930s had become a little less pronounced. They are the inheritors of a securely entrenched and immensely powerful regime. They undoubtedly want change and material improvement, but they will not abandon the system that brought them to prominence to achieve these ends. Although they cannot be considered children of the Russian Revolution, they are very much products of the party that engineered that cataclysmic event.

German political philosopher Karl Marx, whose writings constitute the basis of modern communism. Expelled from Germany in 1849 for publishing his revolutionary opinions, Marx settled in London, where, in 1895, his colleague Friedrich Engels brought to completion the final volume of *Das Kapital* (*Capital*), Marx's massive treatise on politics and economics.

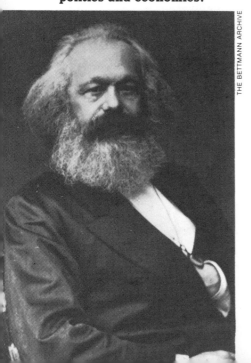

The CPSU cannot be properly understood unless one knows something of its origins. The fact that it is the only political party in the Soviet Union and runs the entire country in a manner that few Westerners would consider even remotely democratic has much to do with the conditions under which the Party came into being, achieved its revolutionary goals, and then defended its gains.

The political organization that eventually became known as the CPSU (originally called the Russian Social-Democratic Labor party, or the RSDLP) was founded in 1898. The program devised by the nine left-wing radicals who founded the organization was based on the writings of the 19th-century German economist and political philosopher Karl Marx, who held that the replacement of capitalism (the economic system under which the means of production — i.e. the land and the factories — are privately owned) by communism (the economic system under which the means of production are owned by the community as a whole) was inevitable. Marx also believed that the transition from capitalism to communism could only be accomplished by revolution.

In accordance with Marx's teachings, the RSDLP called for a two-stage revolution in Russia. In the first stage, Russia's autocratic *tsarist* (imperial) monarchy would be overthrown and the country reconstituted as a democracy. Also during the first stage, the country's industrial base would be expanded and developed by the *bourgeoisie* — the social class that Marx's colleague Friedrich Engels defined as "the class of modern capitalists, owners of the means of social production and employers of wage labor." In the second stage, the Russian *proletariat*, or working class, would overthrow the bourgeoisie, abandon bourgeois democracy and its institutions, and establish socialism — the egalitarian social order that Marx considered the direct precursor of communism.

Since the majority of Russian radicals lived in constant fear of being arrested by the tsarist secret police, the RSDLP, like many other similar organizations, conducted most of its activities abroad. At the RSDLP's second congress, which was held in

Vladimir Ilich Lenin, architect of the Russian Revolution of 1917 and founding father of the Soviet state, addresses a crowd in Petrograd (now Leningrad) in November 1917.

The theory of the communists may be summed up in the single sentence: Abolition of private property.
—KARL MARX
German economist and founder of communism

Two young Soviet citizens read the latest edition of *Pravda* (*Truth*), the official CPSU newspaper, at a public display board in Moscow. State control of the media and all other cultural institutions has been an integral feature of the Soviet system since its inception.

London in 1903, disagreements about the nature of the party caused a major split in its ranks. Lenin declared that the overthrow of the tsarist regime could only be achieved by disciplined and committed revolutionaries who would be prepared to take orders from a central leadership. However, the party members grouped around Yulii Martov, Lenin's main rival, wanted to have the party open to all who supported its program. When the matter was put to a vote, Lenin's faction won, and thus became known as the *Bolsheviks*, or majority. Martov's followers, who became known as the *Mensheviks*, or minority, responded to their defeat by refusing to serve on the party's central committee.

The repercussions of the Bolshevik-Menshevik controversy are still being felt. Bolshevism (which is often used synonymously with Leninism) remains a major component of Marxism-Leninism — the guiding philosophy of the CPSU — to this day. Gorbachev, like his predecessors, ascribes to Marxism-Leninism.

The Bolsheviks believed that their main role was to bring Marxist revolutionary theory and experience to the proletariat. The proletariat would thus learn the class-consciousness that it would need to overthrow the bourgeoisie. Under the Bolshevik system, decisionmaking was, and still is, based on a principle called "democratic centralism," which has been defined by British political scientist David

Lane: "Members participate in the formation of policy and in the election of leaders," he writes, ". . . but when policy has been decided all members are responsible for carrying it out. Only in this way . . . can the party be an effective weapon of the proletariat in its struggle with the bourgeoisie."

The Russian Revolution of November 1917 was actually the second, and most critical, of the two revolutions that took place in that fateful year. The first revolution, which erupted in March, was fueled by popular discontent with the tsarist regime's mismanagement of the Russian war effort. (Russia, allied with France and Great Britain, had been at war with Germany since 1914.) The threat posed to the regime by the riots and strikes that broke out in Petrograd (as Leningrad was then known) on March 7 became even greater on March 10, when troops called in to quell the disturbances refused to fire upon the protesters and joined them instead.

The political ineptitude displayed by Nicholas II, the last *tsar* (emperor) of Russia, and his wife, the Tsarina Alexandra, alienated the vast majority of their subjects and greatly contributed to their downfall. In 1917 Nicholas, faced with increasingly widespread popular opposition to his rule, abdicated on the advice of his ministers.

The tsarist parliament responded by appointing a provisional government, which secured the abdication of Tsar Nicholas II on March 15. The old order was collapsing fast, and the Bolsheviks, in alliance with the Mensheviks and a political party known as the Social-Revolutionaries, were determined to exploit the revolutionary potential of the situation. The three parties were largely instrumental in the creation of the Petrograd *Soviet* (council) of Workers' and Soldiers' Deputies. (The vast difference between Soviet and Western concepts of democracy begins to emerge when one realizes that the soviet, which was to become the basic unit of Soviet democracy, was originally regarded by Lenin as "not a workers' parliament," but as "a fighting organization for the attainment of definite ends.") The Petrograd soviet's opposition to the provisional government intensified in April, when Lenin, who had been living in exile in Switzerland since 1907, arrived in Petrograd, condemned the "capitalists" in the provisional government in a speech to the soviet, and declared that the revolution should continue on to socialism. Lenin was also convinced that the main task now confronting the Party was to educate the masses so that the Bolsheviks would gain a majority in the soviet. The ultimate goal of the Party, he had written, was to be, "Not a parliamentary republic . . . but a republic of soviets of workers', poor peasants', and peasants' deputies throughout the country growing from below upwards."

The struggle between the Petrograd soviet and the provisional government continued throughout the summer of 1917, and culminated in the second revolution, which took place on November 6–7. Lenin and the Bolsheviks staged an almost bloodless uprising against the provisional government and established the Council of People's Commissars as the country's new executive body.

In March 1918 the revolutionary government signed a peace treaty with Germany, thus ending Russia's participation in World War I. Russia's former allies, who had not been consulted by the revolutionary government, immediately moved to aid the Russian army formations that had not gone over to the Bolsheviks. The Bolshevik forces (which were known as the Red Army) fought the counterrevolutionary "White" armies and their Ukrainian, French, British, American, Finnish, and Japanese allies for three years, finally emerging victorious in 1920.

During the civil war the Bolsheviks instituted a program called War Communism. Democratic decision making by the soviets was dispensed with in favor of tighter central controls. A state police force (known as the Cheka) was established to hunt down saboteurs, spies, and counterrevolutionaries. It developed into an extremely powerful instrument of repression, eventually becoming something of a law

An early 20th-century photograph shows a typical Russian peasant village of the period. The characteristics and conditions of the Russian peasantry had barely changed between the 16th and early 20th centuries, which created immense problems for Lenin and the Bolsheviks. The naturally conservative peasants reacted with hostility to proposals for the modernization of agriculture.

NOVOSTI FROM SOVFOTO

Women march in support of the revolution in 1917. The government established by the Bolshevik party (which was reconstituted as the Russian Communist party in 1918 — the forerunner of the CPSU) abolished legal discrimination between the sexes; men and women gained equal privileges and obligations, including the right to vote and to sue for divorce.

unto itself. By 1923, when the Russian Soviet Federated Socialist Republic and the other soviet socialist republics established by the Bolsheviks throughout the former territories of the Russian Empire united as the USSR, the entire country had become a garrison state, and the Soviet leadership had come to believe that the reintroduction of democracy would undermine the political stability that had been achieved by repression.

The adversarial nature that Soviet communism acquired during its formative years, when the Soviet Union was under near-constant political and military siege, was made worse by the fact that many governments refused to recognize the legitimacy of the Soviet regime. Great Britain, for example, did not grant the USSR diplomatic recognition until 1924. The U.S. government did not appoint an ambassador to Moscow until 1933. Yugoslavia, which welcomed thousands of White army supporters, did not recognize the USSR until 1940. Some government officials and political commentators in those noncommunist countries that do have diplomatic relations with the USSR still question the legitimacy of the Soviet regime. For as long as this situation continues, Soviet leaders — and Gorbachev will be no exception — will do everything they can to earn the respect of their critics.

As general secretary of the CPSU, Gorbachev is the leader of an organization dedicated to achieving communism in the Soviet Union and to defending the socialist project and the Soviet people against all threats as the Party perceives them. Like all other Party members, he is supposed to exhibit party-mindedness — a combination of puritanical discipline and singularity of purpose.

Gorbachev has been a team player in the party. He rose quietly through the ranks and seemed suddenly to surface in a position of prominence, displaying all the characteristics of what Westerners would describe as a born politician. He and his colleagues are already better acquainted with the West than their predecessors ever were. They want their citizens to enjoy higher living standards and greater access to a wider variety of consumer goods, but they are unlikely to abandon the state regulation of industry that is the cornerstone of Soviet-type economic systems. Gorbachev and his colleagues have no intention of changing the system; they are, instead, committed to making it more efficient and to enhancing its credibility at home and abroad. And Mikhail Gorbachev's story reveals that he is probably better suited than any of his peers to leading his Party and his country through the radical transformations that will have to be effected if these goals are to be achieved.

Democracy for an insignificant minority, democracy for the rich — that is the democracy of capitalistic society.
—VLADIMIR ILICH LENIN
architect of the Russian Revolution and Soviet leader

Demonstrators in Petrograd flee for their lives as troops loyal to the provisional government open fire in July 1917. Three months earlier Lenin had declared his conviction that all power should reside with the workers' revolutionary *soviets*, or councils.

UPI/BETTMANN NEWSPHOTOS

2

A Man from the Country

Mikhail Sergeevich Gorbachev was born on March 2, 1931, in Privolnoye, a small village near Stavropol, which is one of the largest cities in the southern Soviet Union's Caucasus region. His father, Sergei Andreevich Gorbachev, was an agricultural mechanic. In his son's official *Biographical Outline*, which was published in the fall of 1985, Sergei Gorbachev is described as a man whose ". . . competence in his job, his careful husbandry, his party-inspired sense of justice and his personal modesty earned him universal respect." The same official publication describes Gorbachev's mother thus: "Maria Panteleevna [Gorbachev] was and still is . . . hard-working, and at the age of 74 refuses to leave her native village." The opening sentence of the *Biographical Outline* reflects the fact that a working-class background is still considered not just appropriate, but almost essential, for a senior Soviet official: "Gorbachev's parents," it reads, "were genuine peasants who had to earn their daily bread by the sweat of their brows."

The region where Gorbachev was born bears many resemblances to the American West. It was

> *You cannot make a revolution with silk gloves.*
> —JOSEPH STALIN
> Soviet leader

Joseph Stalin, dictator of the Soviet Union from 1929 until his death in 1953, converses with Lenin in 1922. Stalin, whose memory Gorbachev is known to detest, greatly prized this photograph and often contended that his previous close association with Lenin justified his political supremacy.

Stalin's first Five Year Plan (1929—34) for the modernization of Soviet industry and agriculture was characterized by a dogmatic insistence on production. Here, in 1932, workers on a collective farm near Tashkent, the capital of the Uzbek Soviet Socialist Republic (one of the USSR's 15 constituent republics), try two of their comrades for poor work performance.

first permanently settled toward the end of the 19th century. Over the years, it has attracted a wide variety of different peoples — Armenians, Greeks, Georgians, and others, as well as Russians like the Gorbachevs. The rolling hills and river valleys of the Caucasus also became home to a semi-nomadic people known as the Cossacks, who, like the cowboys of the United States, were expert riders and herdsmen, fiercely attached to the pioneering way of life.

The Gorbachev family was far from rich, and life was difficult for them. Times were especially hard in the 1930s because the Soviet government, led by Joseph Stalin, had initiated a massive campaign to bring all agriculture in the Soviet Union under state control. The country's peasants were systematically herded onto huge, state-run farms, or collectives, which the government believed would be more efficient and productive. Stalin and his colleagues hoped that collectivization would provide the Soviet

Union with enormous agricultural surpluses that could be exported to finance the large-scale industrial expansion called for in the Five Year Plan, the government program for the modernization of industry and agriculture.

Stalin's collectivization campaign was originally aimed mainly at the country's prosperous private farmers, who were known as *kulaks*. However, as peasant resistance to government policy stiffened, the government began to apply the term kulak to all individuals who resisted collectivization. A large proportion of the millions of angry peasants who burned their crops, slaughtered their livestock, and destroyed their farm implements before "joining" the collectives were either killed or imprisoned or deported to the most remote and inhospitable areas of the country. An idea of the scale of the peasants' resistance to collectivization can be gained from the following figures. Between 1928 and 1934, the number of cattle in the Soviet Union fell from 66.8 million to 33.5 million; the number of horses from 36.1 million to 15.4 million; the number of hogs from 27.7 million to 11.5 million; and the number of sheep and goats from 114.6 million to 36.5 million.

The desperate situation created by the peasants' resistance to collectivization became even worse when the government, determined to meet its export targets despite the fact that the country's ag-

An immense bucket of molten ore dwarfs workers at a steel plant built under the first Five Year Plan. The ideological frenzy that accompanied the Soviet drive for industrial expansion and modernization often led to disaster: many new structures, erected against government-imposed deadlines, collapsed before completion.

ricultural resources had already been severely depleted, sent agents into the countryside to levy grain from the peasants by force. That the peasants were often left with insufficient produce to feed themselves was of no interest to the authorities in Moscow. Between 5 million and 10 million people are estimated to have died in the famine that resulted from the collectivization campaign.

The Gorbachevs were undoubtedly affected by the social and economic upheavals that rocked the Soviet Union during the early 1930s. The second half of the decade was also a traumatic period, but for different reasons.

On December 1, 1934, Stalin's chief deputy in Leningrad, Sergei Mironovich Kirov, was assassinated by a young local communist. Some historians believe Kirov to have been a potential rival of Stalin, and therefore suspect that he was killed on Stalin's orders. Stalin probably feared Kirov's considerable prestige and abilities, and undoubtedly resented the

A young Ukrainian woman takes part in a Soviet educational program. Free public education, which had been a major element of Bolshevik proposals for social reform in 1917, fast became a reality following the end of the civil war in 1920, increasing literacy throughout the country to levels undreamed of in the tsarist era.

fact that Kirov had been making speeches that contained a measure of criticism of the collectivization program.

Stalin used Kirov's assassination as evidence of a conspiracy against the Party leadership and proceeded to order the trial and imprisonment or execution of vast numbers of what he and his supporters called "enemies of the people," "wreckers," and "saboteurs." The majority of the victims of Stalin's purge were innocent of their alleged crimes. Thousands of veteran Bolsheviks were executed, along with 35,000 Red Army officers (roughly half the army's officer corps). Historians have calculated that as many as 7 million arrests may have been made by the Soviet secret police (which had been renamed the People's Commissariat of Internal Affairs, or NKVD) between 1936 and 1938 alone, and that about 3 million people died, either through execution or through being worked to death in forced-labor camps.

The Stavropol area did not escape the upheavals caused by Stalin's purge, and there were still NKVD units stationed in the Caucasus at the end of the 1930s.

In 1941, when Gorbachev was 10 years old, the Soviet Union found itself facing the greatest crisis in its history when Germany reneged on the non-aggression treaty that had been negotiated by Stalin and Adolf Hitler, the German head of state, in August 1939. The Germans invaded on June 22, 1941, taking the Red Army by surprise, and the Soviet Union became the scene of some of the bloodiest battles in history. The Soviet people, still demoralized by the social and economic disasters that had befallen them during the 1930s, were mobilized to stem the German advance.

German forces first appeared in the northern Caucasus in the summer of 1942. Their objective was to slice through the region and move on southward to seize the oil fields around Baku, in southern Georgia. The Germans also hoped that securing the Caucasus would enable them to exert pressure on neighboring Turkey (which had been allied with Germany in World War I) to abandon its neutrality

Following the German invasion of the USSR in 1941, the production of military equipment and materials was accorded top priority throughout Soviet industry. This propaganda poster from 1942 stresses the important role that female workers played in war production.

TASS FROM SOVFOTO

Soviet troops in action at Stalingrad in December 1942, when the Soviet forces were beginning to recover from the terrible reverses they had suffered during the first year of the conflict. Few of the 91,000 Germans who surrendered at Stalingrad in January 1943 ever returned home, since the Soviets treated German captives as barbarically as the Germans did Soviet prisoners.

and support Germany again. The cooperation of the Turks would greatly aid Germany's efforts to gain supremacy in the eastern Mediterranean and the Middle East.

The German occupation of the Stavropol area was relatively brief. Before the Germans could consolidate their position, they were forced to withdraw. In January 1943 Soviet forces inflicted a crushing defeat on the German Sixth Army at Stalingrad, a city to the northeast of Stavropol. Had the German army remained in Stavropol, it would have been in great danger of being outflanked by the Soviet advance.

The Soviet victory at Stalingrad was the beginning of the end for the Germans. The Red Army pushed Hitler's forces back across eastern Europe and entered Berlin, the German capital, early in 1945. More than 20 million Soviet citizens had lost their lives in the conflict.

For the Gorbachev family, the end of the war meant a return to the way of life they had known previously. Mikhail resumed his education in the local schools. His father was demobilized and returned to work as a mechanic on a collective. Years later, Gorbachev said that his father had always encouraged him to study and work hard, and that this had helped him lay the foundations of his future success.

Gorbachev and his fellow students at the high

Soviet peasants return to their village following its liberation from the Germans in February 1943. Soviet war losses, both military and civilian, were appalling: by 1945, when the Soviet capture of Berlin, the German capital, brought the conflict to an end, 20 million Soviet citizens had died, and one-quarter of the nation's property had been destroyed.

SOVFOTO

school he attended were frequently required to take temporary leaves of absence to help bring in the harvest. Gorbachev later recalled that he had once driven a combine harvester with no cab for hours on end in bitterly cold weather. Finally, to ward off at least the worst of the cold, he wrapped himself in straw that he had gathered from the field, and pressed on with his task.

In 1950 Gorbachev received his first opportunity to broaden his horizons. It was in that year that he left Stavropol to study law at Moscow State University. At that time, admission to Moscow State University, the most prestigious seat of learning in the country, was usually reserved for the best students, or for sons and daughters of the country's most prominent leaders. Gorbachev was undoubtedly intelligent and hard-working, but he does not seem to have had the kind of political connections that would have guaranteed him admission. Although he did obtain recommendations from politicians and civic organizations in the Stavropol area, he seems to have secured entry to the university mainly as a result of his own efforts. However, a small proportion of the places available at the university were reserved for members of minority groups, for those with peasant or worker backgrounds, and for stu-

Moscow's Kremlin, where Stalin remained for much of the time following the German invasion. The first disastrous months of the German invasion almost broke the Soviet dictator, who responded to the situation by drinking heavily and making life impossible for his staff.

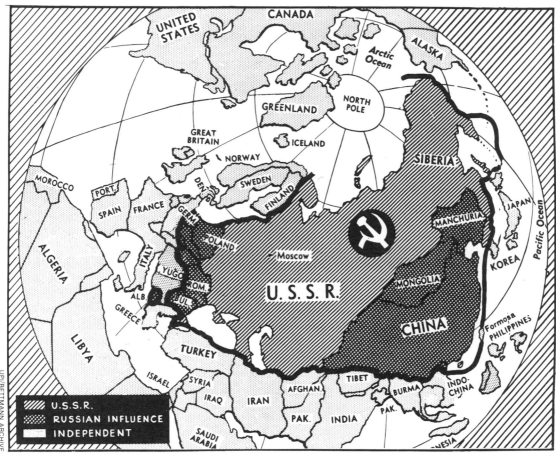

U.S.S.R.
RUSSIAN INFLUENCE
INDEPENDENT

A map shows the extent of Soviet political mastery in the world at the time of Stalin's death in 1953.

dents from remote areas. Gorbachev would certainly have qualified for admission on the second and third counts.

Gorbachev traveled the several hundred miles from Stavropol to Moscow by train. Later, he recalled that the journey had affected him profoundly. Despite the enormous efforts that had been made to repair the damage caused by the war, the devastation wrought by the German invasion was still visible throughout the Soviet Union. The combined effects of the loss of manpower during the war years and Stalin's postwar policies, which favored heavy industry and military programs and ignored needs of the ordinary Soviet citizen, meant that comparatively little had been done to rebuild homes and restore basic amenities. Even as late as 1950, the scars of war were still fresh in the cities through which young Gorbachev rode. The extent of the damage shocked and dismayed him.

In Moscow, Gorbachev was enrolled in the law faculty at the university. Law was an unusual choice in Stalin's time, because it was not seen as a standard avenue to a successful career. The official emphasis on rebuilding the country's industrial base and improving Soviet military technology made qualifications in the natural sciences a much better guarantee of social advancement than qualifications in nontechnical subjects.

The university, situated in the heart of Moscow, afforded a view of the Kremlin, where Stalin and many other major figures who had participated in the founding of the Soviet state lived and worked. Here, Gorbachev could feel that he had made a huge leap from his beginnings in remote, provincial Stavropol. Although he was not a particularly outstanding student, he did achieve prominence as a singularly fervent campus politician.

The recollections of those who knew Gorbachev at the university tend to focus on the fact that he was a devoted member of the *Komsomol*, or Young Communist League. Open to everyone between the ages of 14 and 28, the Komsomol is designed to fill the gap between the Pioneers (roughly equivalent to the Boy Scouts and Girl Scouts) and full membership in the Communist party. Since Komsomol activities can take up a great deal of a member's time, only a small number of students — usually those with political ambitions — become really prominent. The Komsomol is closely controlled by the Party, and Komsomol members are often used by the Party as propagandists for official programs and campaigns. Komsomol members are also expected to donate much of their time to taking part in construction projects, or helping with the harvest whenever labor is in short supply. It is from the dedicated Komsomol members that the Soviet regime usually recruits its new officials.

The 20-year-old Gorbachev was quick to recognize the importance of political connections. He became

> *[I remember] the steely voice of the Komsomol secretary of the law faculty, Gorbachev, demanding expulsion from the Komsomol for the slightest offense, from inappropriately telling political anecdotes to shirking being sent to a kolkhoz [collective farm].*
> —FRIDRIKH NEZNANSKY
> Soviet émigré and novelist, on fellow student Gorbachev

a vigorous Komsomol activist who, according to one acquaintance, "just loved to make speeches." By the time Gorbachev reached his senior year, in 1954, he had been elected head of the Komsomol organization at Moscow State University. He had already become a member of the CPSU in 1952, and it seemed likely, even at this early stage, that he would eventually pursue a career in the Party apparatus.

At that time, Stalin was still very much alive and in control, and there were indications that the suspicious and aging dictator was preparing yet another purge of Party and government officials. Then, on March 5, 1953, Stalin died. A new era in the history of the Soviet Union had dawned. There would be many opportunities for bright young Party loyalists like Gorbachev as the political infighting that followed Stalin's death and eventually brought Nikita Khrushchev to power as first secretary of the CPSU took its toll of those politicians who had opposed Khrushchev's rise to supremacy.

Soviet Prime Minister Nikolai Bulganin (top right) votes for his own removal from office at a Central Committee meeting on March 27, 1958. Bulganin was succeeded as prime minister by Nikita Khrushchev (front row, center) first secretary of the CPSU, who was also appointed chairman of the nation's Supreme Defense Council. Khrushchev thus gained complete control of the state, the Party, and the military.

3

From the Farm to the Capital

Given his record at the university and in the Komsomol, Gorbachev hoped that, following graduation, he would be offered employment in the central bureaucracy in Moscow, where the greatest opportunities seemed to lie. However, fate and the CPSU decreed otherwise. In 1955 Gorbachev was sent back to Stavropol, where he was given the rather minor position of deputy head of the Agitation and Propaganda department in the Komsomol's Stavropol City Committee. Gorbachev was accompanied to Stavropol by his wife, Raisa Maksimovna, a philosophy graduate.

In those days, Stavropol was still very much a farming community. Life revolved around the market square, where farmers with mud on their boots and callouses on their hands came to sell their produce and to socialize. Eventually, however, the square would lose its rustic aspect; it would be ringed with modern buildings housing Party and government offices. Gorbachev was to play an important part in modernizing Stavropol and its surrounding regions.

UPI/BETTMANN NEWSPHOTOS

Testifying before the U.S. Senate Armed Services Committee in March 1962, shortly after he was released from prison in the Soviet Union, American airman Francis Gary Powers displays a model of the U-2 high-altitude reconnaissance aircraft he was flying when he was shot down over the USSR in 1960. The incident triggered a major political crisis and seriously damaged U.S.-Soviet relations.

Soviet Premier Nikita Khrushchev addresses the General Assembly of the United Nations on September 23, 1960. Khrushchev's lapse into such extremes of indecorum as fist-pounding and shoe-banging — common gestures of disapproval among the Russian peasantry — shocked the gathered diplomats and reinforced the contention of his conservative opponents within the CPSU that his flamboyance made him a political liability.

UPI/BETTMANN NEWSPHOTOS

Workers in Poznan, Poland, protest the repressive policies of their country's ruling party, the Soviet-backed Polish United Workers party (PZPR), in June 1956. Popular disaffection with the pro-Moscow communist regimes established by the Soviet government in eastern Europe remains a major cause of concern to the Soviet leadership.

In the late 1950s, Gorbachev was just one of thousands of minor Party officials in the northern Caucasus. In 1956 he was appointed secretary of the Komsomol in the Stavropol region. In 1958 he was promoted to first secretary, a post that gave him supervisory authority over the Komsomol organization not just in Stavropol, but throughout the whole northern Caucasus. In 1962 he finally joined the Party machine, as organizer of the territorial production management of all collective and state farms in the Stavropol region. It was an important job because grain production provided most of the area's income. Eager to carry out his duties as effectively as possible, Gorbachev enrolled in a correspondence course in agronomy at the Stavropol Agricultural Institute, adding theoretical knowledge to the practical experience of farming that he had gained during his childhood. In his new position,

Gorbachev emerged as a motivated and energetic administrator. As German journalist and Soviet affairs expert Christian Schmidt-Häuer writes in his book *Gorbachev: The Path to Power*, "Gorbachev was . . . quite unlike those old-style [agitation and propaganda] officials who . . . sit behind green baize tables . . . issuing stereotyped appeals to the masses. Gorbachev was a novelty — a manager who made independent decisions and drew his own conclusions."

Gorbachev was clearly a man on the move. Further proof of the fact that he had been singled out for advancement came in December 1962, when he was appointed head of the Party Organizations Department in the Stavropol Regional Party Committee. Even in this essentially political position, Gorbachev continued to concern himself with agricultural affairs in the Stavropol region.

Agriculture in the Soviet Union is strictly controlled by the state. Some farmland is set aside for personal use by citizens; but even though these private plots tend to be far more productive than state-owned land, most of the official emphasis is still placed on *sovkhozes* (state farms) and *kolkhozes* (collective farms). (The difference in name refers to the different ways in which the farms are organized. Both types of farm, however, are government-owned operations controlled and supervised by the Party.)

Hungarian freedom fighters patrol the streets of Budapest, the Hungarian capital, on November 4, 1956, shortly before Soviet forces intervened to crush the anti-Soviet rebellion that had erupted throughout Hungary two weeks earlier. The Red Army's brutal repression of the Hungarian uprising severely impaired the international standing of the Soviet government.

Khrushchev meets with workers on a collective farm in the Kazakh Soviet Socialist Republic in 1956. Khrushchev was determined to make the Soviet Union's agricultural system — which is state-controlled — as efficient and sophisticated as the market-oriented agrosystems of the West.

Under Khrushchev there was a partial restoration of legality, the elimination of brutal terror, and rehabilitation of millions of victims.
—ZHORES A. MEDVEDEV
Soviet émigré and historian

Before the revolution, farming in Russia had largely been in the hands of the peasants and the landowners. The peasants plowed the land, seeded it, and reaped the harvest; the landowners took most of the profits. Although some attempts had been made to improve the peasants' situation during the 19th century, their living conditions were still pitiful when the Russian Revolution occurred.

In fact, many modern historians believe that the nature, beliefs, characteristics, and conditions of the Russian peasantry barely changed between the 16th and early 20th centuries. It is not surprising that the peasants usually became ardent supporters of those who promised change. However, when the revolutionary government failed to deliver on the promises it had made, the peasants rebelled against the new regime, eventually provoking Stalin into ordering collectivization in a last desperate attempt to bring agriculture under government control. Stalin, however, was far from progressive in his agricultural policies. He may have paid lip service to modernization and mechanization, but in fact he sought mainly to extract as much as possible from the farms, while investing as little as possible in improving them. Not until Stalin died and was succeeded by Nĭkita Khrushchev did Soviet agriculture begin to become more advanced.

Khrushchev was a native of the Ukraine, one of the most important grain-producing areas in the entire country, and he lobbied to increase the amount of money spent on agricultural machinery, fertilizer, and other essentials.

It was during the Khrushchev years that Gorbachev had become chief of the agriculture department for the Stavropol region. While Gorbachev had been working to improve agricultural production, Khrushchev had been trying, in his own highly erratic and individualistic way, to boost agricultural output throughout the Soviet Union. He had become notorious for his readiness to try any scheme that caught his fancy, often initiating policy programs that, though undoubtedly adventurous, were often ill conceived. In fact, Khrushchev was one of the most unusual — and colorful — leaders the Soviet Union ever had.

Khrushchev, like many of his colleagues, was a political opportunist of the first order, but he was also more than that. Although he had received only the most rudimentary education, his native intelligence and cunning enabled him to rise above his contemporaries in the Party and in the regime. As British historian Edward Crankshaw writes in his book: *Khrushchev: A Career*, Nikita Khrushchev

Walter Ulbricht (at podium), head of state of the German Democratic Republic, is applauded by the Soviet leadership at the Twenty-Second Congress of the CPSU, October 1961. At this congress, Khrushchev, continuing the de-Stalinization campaign initiated in 1956, ordered Stalin's remains removed from their place of honor in the Lenin Mausoleum.

"... achieved his eminence at a time when success could be obtained only by atrocious methods and over the dead or broken bodies of innumerable comrades."

As first secretary of the CPSU, Khrushchev worked feverishly to realize his ambitions for the Soviet Union. Following his first visit to the United States, he became almost obsessed with surpassing America in every conceivable way. His determination to prove what he considered the inherent superiority of the socialist system gave rise to many memorable pronouncements, perhaps the most famous of which was contained in a speech he made to the Polish Communist party in 1956. "I say this to the capitalist states," he declared, "... it doesn't depend on you whether or not we exist. ... Whether you like it or not history is on our side. We will bury you."

Despite the fact that Khrushchev made many enemies within the Soviet hierarchy, at the height of his power he had become almost a dictator.

One of Khrushchev's most famous initiatives was his plan to cultivate the so-called "Virgin Lands" of Soviet Central Asia. In 1954 he proposed that these grasslands, which had lain idle for centuries and were used only by nomads to provide forage for their herds of sheep and cattle, be plowed, and sown with grain and corn. In theory, this was a good idea — except for one detail which Khrushchev chose to ignore. The rainfall in the area was notoriously uncertain. One year there might be plenty of rain; successive years might bring drought. Khrushchev overrode all objections, however. His boorish attitude and his fixation with introducing corn as a crop caused him to be nicknamed *"Kukuriznitsa,"* which means "cornball" or "country bumpkin" in Russian. Thousands of Soviet citizens, among them many Komsomol work brigades, were mobilized to begin the great task of converting the grasslands into a major source of grain crops. The experiment was a great success at first, but, like many similar agricultural projects in the Soviet Union, failed to live up to initial expectations. With improved irrigation, however, some of the areas involved are now

In October 1962, shortly after he was informed by his military intelligence chiefs that Soviet nuclear missiles had been installed in Cuba and would soon be fully operational, U.S. President John F. Kennedy signed a proclamation ordering a naval blockade of Cuba to prevent further shipments of Soviet weaponry from reaching the island.

MISSILE ERECTOR

CABLE

MISSILE SHELTER TENT

TRACKED PRIME MOVERS

OXIDIZER TANK TRAILERS

FUEL TANK TRAILERS

consistently proving productive.

Khrushchev's blunt and forthright manners eventually came to alienate many Soviet officials and citizens alike. They would have preferred a leader capable of communicating the Soviet position to the world in a more statesmanlike manner, a leader capable of showing sophistication and serenity. Khrushchev's denunciation of Stalin, which he made in February 1956, during his address to the Twentieth Congress of the CPSU, and his subsequent introduction of moderate reforms created a rising tide of expectations among his supporters, expectations that were not to be fulfilled. Khrushchev's agricultural failures finally prompted his longtime opponents and supporters alike to join forces and work toward removing him from power. Many high officials in the Party and the government thought Khrushchev's schemes "harebrained," and began openly to quarrel with him. One of the most prominent of Khrushchev's critics was Fedor Kulakov.

An October 23, 1962, U.S. Defense Department photograph shows Soviet missile sites under construction at San Cristóbal, Cuba. The Soviet attempt to station nuclear weapons in the Caribbean failed. On October 28 Khrushchev, faced with American intransigence and under pressure from the majority of his colleagues, who considered him guilty of adventurism, ordered the missiles withdrawn.

AP/WIDE WORLD PHOTOS

Mikhail Suslov, who was for many years one of the CPSU's leading ideologists, was the main architect of Khrushchev's ouster in 1964. Suslov continued to hold influential positions and, during the late 1970s, was one of Gorbachev's most powerful patrons.

In the early years of Khrushchev's administration, Kulakov had been one of his most ardent supporters, but had eventually fallen foul of Khrushchev's notorious temper. In 1960 he was removed from the central bureaucracy and demoted to the relatively obscure post of Party secretary for the Stavropol region. Kulakov was an astute politician, however, and he took care to maintain the connections he had made in Moscow.

The region around Stavropol is famous for its health resorts, which each summer attract some of the most prominent politicians in the Soviet Union. During Kulakov's time these included First Deputy Prime Minister Aleksei Kosygin, Yuri Andropov (head of the Central Committee's foreign affairs department), and Mikhail Suslov (a Politburo member since 1952 and the CPSU's chief ideologist). Andropov and Suslov were already acquainted with the region. Andropov had been born there and Suslov had served there during the war with Germany, when, as the local Party secretary, he had been instrumental in organizing partisan fighting units that operated with much success behind German lines. Kosygin, Andropov, and Suslov were all friendly with Kulakov, and increasingly disturbed by what they saw as the erratic and dangerous behavior of Khrushchev. Although it is certain that some of the plotting that eventually toppled Khrushchev took place in the Stavropol region, Gorbachev was probably too junior an official to have had a share in these schemes.

In the fall of 1964, Khrushchev was on vacation at his retreat on the Black Sea. On October 14 he was conferring with a visiting French statesman when he received a telephone call from Leonid Brezhnev, his deputy and, as president of the Presidium of the Supreme Soviet (the Soviet parliament), Soviet head of state. Brezhnev requested that Khrushchev return to the capital for an urgent meeting of the Central Committee. Khrushchev knew that the supposed subject of the meeting — the reorganization of agriculture — scarcely required him to cut his vacation short. However, when Brezhnev then informed him that the Central Committee would simply make decisions in his absence if he failed to return, Khrushchev ordered a plane to be sent to fetch him immediately.

Upon his return to Moscow, Khrushchev was promptly voted out of office. Suslov, who was one of the key figures in the affair, delivered a searing speech denouncing Khrushchev's policies at the climactic meeting of the Central Committee that brought about the first secretary's downfall. Khrushchev is the only Soviet leader ever to have been ousted from power.

The new general secretary of the Party was Brezhnev. During Stalin's final years, Brezhnev had appeared to be one of those being groomed by the aging dictator to replace the old guard. After Stalin's death, he had at first seemed to fade from public view, but he had gradually worked his way back into the central leadership.

It was not long before Kulakov was also brought back to Moscow. In September 1965, about a year after his return to the city, he was named Central Committee secretary for agriculture. Andropov was also promoted to a position of real importance. In May 1967, after 10 years of service in the Central Committee, he was appointed head of the Committee for State Security, the Soviet secret police, an organization familiarly known by its Russian initials — the KGB. Along with Suslov, these men were

SOVFOTO

Soviet President Leonid I. Brezhnev signs a decree ratifying the Nuclear Test Ban Treaty (whose other signatories were Great Britain and the United States) at a ceremony in the Kremlin on September 25, 1963. Looking on is one of Brezhnev's most trusted aides, Politburo member Konstantin U. Chernenko, who was appointed general secretary of the CPSU in 1984.

45

now in positions of power, from which they could easily promote the careers of their supporters.

While stationed in Stavropol, Kulakov had formed a very high opinion of Gorbachev, considering him the ablest of the regional Party officials concerned with agriculture. And Kulakov must have approved, if not initiated, Gorbachev's promotion in 1966 to the post of first secretary of the Communist party of the city of Stavropol. After holding that post for two years, Gorbachev was appointed second secretary of the Stavropol regional Party committee. Two years later, in 1970, he again moved up the ladder to become first secretary of the regional Party committee. It was typical of Gorbachev that during what must have been a time of intense Party activity, he had still found the time to complete his correspondence course in agronomy at the Stavropol Agricultural Institute, graduating as a "scientific agricultural economist" in 1967.

In addition to advancing in regional positions, Gorbachev began making his way into the more influential central organization of the Party. In 1970 he also became a deputy to the Council of the Union of the Supreme Soviet of the USSR, and subsequently served on several committees of that body. Then, in 1971, came full confirmation of Gorbachev's rise to prominence; he was named a member of the Central Committee of the CPSU. He had been admitted to the inner circle.

There were other signs that the young secretary from Stavropol had risen in the favor of the central authorities. In 1972 Gorbachev made his first trip abroad — a brief visit to Belgium. During the rest of the decade he was to pay similar visits to West Germany (1975), France (1976), and Czechoslovakia (1979). In the Soviet Union it takes a good deal of political influence to be allowed to go abroad, and it is a sign of special prominence to be chosen head of a delegation, as Gorbachev was on several of these occasions.

At the beginning of his incumbency as general secretary, Brezhnev seems to have been a compromise candidate agreed upon by several factions in the top ranks of the Party. These factions differed

Politburo member and Central Committee Secretary for Agriculture Fedor Kulakov — to whose attention Gorbachev came during the early 1960s, when Kulakov was Party chief for the Stavropol region — attends the Eleventh Congress of the Yugoslav Communist party in Belgrade, the Yugoslavian capital, in June 1978. Gorbachev succeeded his patron as Central Committee secretary for agriculture in 1978.

radically on both domestic and foreign policy. As time went on, Brezhnev gradually outmaneuvered his most powerful opponents, thus ensuring his own preeminence. For example, there was originally considerable doubt about the position of Prime Minister Aleksei Kosygin. To some observers, it seemed that Kosygin, and not Brezhnev, was the most powerful figure in the new regime. Kosygin was widely experienced in Kremlin politics. He had first risen to prominence in Leningrad, and then became a deputy premier of the Soviet Union, at age 36, in 1940. In the ensuing years, his career had been somewhat erratic, but had never fallen far enough to remove Kosygin from the center entirely. Nor was Kosygin Brezhnev's only opponent. Gradually, however, Brezhnev overtook the others. By the mid-1970s, Brezhnev was clearly the principal leader of the Soviet Union.

Although Gorbachev may not have been directly involved in these political maneuverings, their results certainly affected his career. People who were later to act as his sponsors — Suslov, Andropov, and, perhaps most importantly, Kulakov — were

Gorbachev [is] a careerist who earned his job the old-fashioned way: by paying court to powerful men.
—*Newsweek,* March 25, 1985

47

deeply enmeshed in these intrigues. An ally of these powerful figures, Gorbachev remained "the good party soldier," a position which would stand him in good stead when his turn came to move one more rung up the ladder.

Foreign events were also unsettling life for the Soviet regime in the late 1960s and early 1970s. There was the age-old boundary dispute with China, and there was the issue of *detente*, or peaceful co-existence, with the West. Brezhnev's pursuit of detente with the United States caused some dissension in the Party and in the regime. Some key military figures, for example, urged a more belligerent policy toward Washington and its allies. But the greatest cause for anxiety was right next door: the increasing discord and the threat of uprisings in the Soviet Union's satellite states — those Eastern European countries liberated from the Germans by the Red Army at the end of World War II and ruled since by Soviet-installed, Soviet-backed communist governments. The most serious threat to Soviet hegemony in Eastern Europe emanated from Czechoslovakia. Matters came to a head in the spring and summer of 1968. To the diehard purists in the Kremlin, the moderate economic and social reforms initiated by the Czechoslovakian Communist party, headed by Alexander Dubček, seemed ideological heresy. The political and nationalistic differences between the two countries intensified until Brezhnev and his colleagues finally decided that what was happening in Czechoslovakia amounted to counterrevolution and that the Soviet Union had no alternative but to invade. To the Kremlin, it seemed that Dubček's policies could only lead to Czechoslovakia's turning its back on its communist neighbors, which would shatter the unity of the Warsaw Pact (the defensive alliance concluded between the USSR and its Eastern European satellites in 1955) and possibly inspire other Eastern European nations to seek increased independence from Moscow.

In August 1968 the Red Army and elements of the armed forces of other Warsaw Pact countries invaded Czechoslovakia and crushed the reformists. The invasion of Czechoslovakia represented the first

Brezhnev brought some element of stability to the Soviet Union, and the predictability of growth.
—ZHORES A. MEDVEDEV
Soviet historian

(and thus far the only) application of what came to be know as the "Brezhnev Doctrine" — a policy formulation that has never been publicly promulgated by the Soviets but whose basic details emerged in a speech that Brezhnev made to Polish communists in November 1968: "[When] internal and external forces, hostile to socialism, seek to reverse the development of any socialist country . . . in the direction of the restoration of the capitalist order . . . this already becomes not only a problem of the people concerned, but also a common problem and the concern of all socialist countries."

While the Soviet hierarchy was preoccupied with keeping its allies in line, Gorbachev was still busy trying to further the fortunes of the Party and the farms in the Stavropol region. Those who knew him at this stage of his career remember him as extremely hard-working and ambitious but at the same time considerate and thoughtful. Something of a sports enthusiast, he was especially interested in amateur boxing. Arkady Shevchenko, the highest-ranking Soviet official to have defected to the West, remembers Gorbachev as a reasonable man, less arrogant — and much more energetic — than the average Party official. Gorbachev had modernized the center of Stavropol and provided better facilities for both the Party and local government administration.

In agricultural matters, Gorbachev's overriding concern was to provide incentives for the farm workers to increase their output. He established a model kolkhoz to showcase the methods he advocated. He also pushed for improved housing and living conditions for farm workers, an aspect of development that had been notoriously neglected in the Soviet Union. (The majority of the rural population continued to live in much the same primitive conditions that had prevailed before Lenin's revolution a half-century earlier.) When a prolonged drought struck the Stavropol region in 1973 and 1974, Gorbachev was especially energetic in obtaining emergency feed supplies for the important sheep- and horse-raising operations around Stavropol. The grateful farmers became his enthusiastic supporters.

UPI/BETTMANN NEWSPHOTOS

Following his appointment to the position of first secretary of the Czechoslovak Communist party in January 1968, Alexander Dubček initiated a reform program that the Soviet government believed would undermine the party's supremacy and pave the way for a restoration of liberal democracy. The Soviet government ordered the Red Army and token Warsaw Pact forces into Czechoslovakia to crush the reform movement on August 20, 1968.

Soviet tanks patrol the streets of Prague, the Czech capital, on September 4, 1968. To reassert their control over Czechoslovakia, the Soviets ordered a massive purge of reformers from the Czech Communist party, the restoration of censorship, and a renewal of emphasis on communist ideology in education and the media.

But then tragedy struck at the center of Soviet politics. On July 18, 1978, Fedor Kulakov, Central Committee secretary for agriculture since 1965 and a Politburo member since 1971, died — according to official reports — of a heart attack. Actually, however, as Schmidt-Häuer explains, ". . . it is now known that [Kulakov] committed suicide; he was found with his wrists cut. There has never been any reliable information about his motives, but at the time of his death rumor had it that he had been at the center of a furious argument in the party."

Since the rise of Brezhnev, Kulakov had again become one of the most prominent men in the Soviet Union. As Central Committee secretary for agriculture, he had held one of the most important —

Brezhnev and U.S. President Richard M. Nixon share a joke at the White House on June 18, 1973. The considerable mutual understanding achieved by Nixon and Brezhnev during the early 1970s resulted in a tangible, though short-lived, reduction of political and military tensions between their two countries.

and difficult — jobs in the entire government bureaucracy. Kulakov's performance in agriculture, although promising, had not been a great success. At Kulakov's funeral in Red Square (which neither Brezhnev, nor Kosygin, nor Suslov attended) Gorbachev was one of the leading official mourners, delivering a eulogy for his dead patron. It was a prominent role for the young man from Stavropol. Gorbachev was on the way to the top.

4

At the Center in Moscow

Kulakov's sudden death created a major hiatus in the capabilities of Soviet leadership. Although several of the most prominent members of the regime, including Brezhnev himself, had strong opinions on how agricultural policy should be handled, none of them had Kulakov's depth of experience in that area. Moreover, in the past the position of Central Committee secretary for agriculture had all too often proven the ruin of promising political careers. None of the Moscow elite seemed particularly eager to take over Kulakov's responsibilities.

It was probably for these reasons that the leadership turned to Gorbachev. Since Kulakov had always spoken highly of his young protegé, Gorbachev's abilities were known to many of the most powerful men in the Kremlin, including Suslov, Andropov, Kosygin, and probably Brezhnev as well. Accordingly, in November 1978, Gorbachev was summoned to Moscow to assume the position of Central Committee agricultural secretary. Gorbachev realized that he would have to work extremely hard and learn fast if he was to compensate for his lack of experience in agriculture at the na-

TASS FROM SOVFOTO

An elderly peasant from the Turkmen Soviet Socialist Republic drinks a toast at celebrations marking the 60th anniversary of the founding of the USSR, which was established by treaty in 1922 and received a constitution in 1924.

A fleet of combine harvesters sweeps across a field in the Kazakh Soviet Socialist Republic in 1972. During the early stages as Central Committee secretary for agriculture, Gorbachev worked hard to compensate for his lack of experience in agriculture at the national level, acquainting himself with regional variations so as to arrive at realistic quota recommendations.

tional level. Ensuring that the less hospitable areas of the Soviet Union achieved their production targets would be far more problematic than experimenting with model kolkhozes in the northern Caucasus, where the climate and the quality of the soil made for reasonably consistent and acceptable levels of productivity.

In many ways, the difficulties facing farmers and agronomists in the Soviet Union have less to do with political or economic considerations than might be imagined. The most critical factors determining the fortunes of Soviet agriculture are climate and geography.

Stavropol, for instance, which is situated in one of the more southerly areas of the country, lies at about the same latitude as North Dakota, in the United States. Kiev, the center of another major grain-producing area, shares approximately the same latitude as Edmonton, in Alberta, Canada. Thus, in the Soviet Union's key farming regions,

A Soviet agricultural economist (foreground, right) answers technical questions concerning cattle-breeding put to him by the *aksakals*, or elders, of a farming community in the Kirghiz Soviet Socialist Republic. The fact that farm workers in the USSR have few incentives to do more work than is absolutely necessary remains a major obstacle to the advancement of agriculture in that country.

Two Soviet agronomists (in light coats) and a shepherd confer at an agricultural experimental station in the Kirghiz Soviet Socialist Republic. Government investment in scientific research aimed at increasing the productivity of land suitable for farming was greatly expanded during the Khrushchev era and remains substantial to this day.

those on which the country relies for grain production, the growing season is much shorter than that of the main farming regions in the United States, Western Europe or Australia. This means that cold weather can threaten crop production at both ends of the production process, interfering with planting and harvesting. In addition, most of the farmland in the Soviet Union lies inland, far from the moderating effects of the oceans. This type of continental climate is notoriously subject to irregular rainfall, in itself a serious obstacle to consistency of productivity. Finally, though the USSR covers a vast expanse of the Eurasian land mass, much of the country is comprised of forest, desert, swamps, and other land unsuitable for farming. The actual area of arable soil is relatively small. Even in good years this is barely enough to provide for the 270 million citizens of the Soviet Union.

The limited viability of Soviet agriculture also has a human dimension. As Gorbachev himself recognized, one of the chief obstacles to the advancement of Soviet agriculture is the fact that farm workers have no incentive to do more than the barest minimum. Why, they argue, should they work from

55

The Ukrainian village of Kodaki is just one of the more than 400,000 rural inhabited localities in the USSR. Government programs to improve the living standards of the rural population were accelerated during the 1970s.

dawn to dusk and (often even longer) when their only reward is dismal living conditions, chronic shortages of many of the material comforts that Westerners take for granted, and little hope of any improvement in the foreseeable future? It must also be mentioned that there remains in some areas, though to no great extent around Stavropol, a residual distrust of the central bureaucracy in Moscow, a distrust that dates back to the collectivization era of the 1930s.

It is against this background, then, that Gorbachev began his new career. The results of the first harvest conducted during his incumbency were fairly heartening. When the statistics for the 1978 harvest were finally compiled, it was estimated that 237 million tons of grain had been produced. But in 1979, the national grain yield dropped catastrophically — to 179 million tons. The figures for 1980 — 189 million tons — were not much of an improvement. As a result, the Soviet Union was forced to use a proportion of its valuable foreign exchange reserves to buy grain from the United States, Canada, and other grain-producing nations.

The 1979 figures for the USSR's gross grain output tell only part of the story. A continuing problem for the Soviet government in addition to the difficulty experienced in growing and harvesting the crop is the sometimes even greater problem of transporting it to the consumers. Inefficient road and rail transportation, combined with poor planning and distribution, often mean interruptions in the food supply that result in shortages in the stores.

NOVOSTI FROM SOVFOTO

Soviet shoppers wait in line at a private farmers' market in Siberia. The quality of the produce grown on the USSR's privately owned farmland (which occupies only four percent of the country's arable land but yields 25 percent of the nation's total agricultural output) is vastly superior to that of the produce grown on state farms.

Kulakov had shown that he was aware of this problem, and Gorbachev attempted to deal with it in his own turn.

For several years now, the Soviet government has been expanding investment in agriculture, and a greater proportion of the nation's industrial capacity has been utilized to boost the quantity and the quality of agricultural equipment and fertilizers. Though this has brought about some moderate increases in per-acre and per-employee productivity, the Soviet farmer is still, by most criteria, much less productive then his American, Canadian, or Australian counterparts. This situation is particularly bizarre (and, to Soviet officials, extremely embarrassing) when one realizes that there is one area of Soviet agriculture that is remarkably productive — the area of private plots. These plots are set aside from the state land, but their use is strictly controlled and limited by the state. Those who work

Communism is mankind's tomorrow.
—LEONID BREZHNEV
Soviet leader

57

these plots do not own the land, but, as long as their work is performed conscientiously and their political records are beyond reproach, they are able to cultivate this land. The amount of land available for private cultivation tends to vary according to the whims of the bureaucrats and their political masters, but those who farm the plots, often by using ingenious equipment of their own devising, have made them vitally important to the Soviet economy.

Any visitor to the Soviet Union is struck by the limited choice and poor quality of the merchandise available in Soviet stores, even in the center of Moscow. This is not the case, however, in the markets where the private farmers sell their produce. The market in Stavropol, for example, has stalls that in the late summer and fall are piled high with the most luscious tomatoes, apples, and other fruits and vegetables.

Although private plots occupy only 4 percent of

Displaying the architectural extravagance typical of Russian Orthodox places of worship, the Preobrazhenskaya Church dominates its surroundings near the Soviet city of Petrozavodsk. Religious freedom, though technically guaranteed under the country's constitution, remains severely limited in the USSR.

SOVFOTO

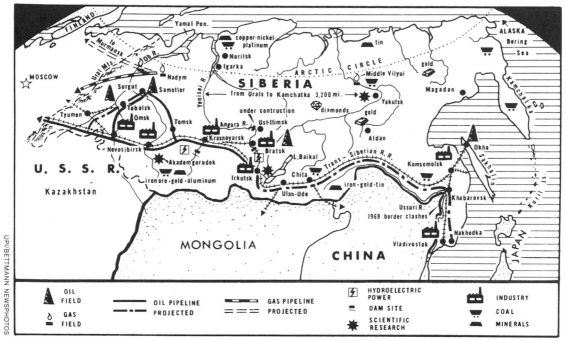

the Soviet Union's arable land, they produce 25 percent of the nation's total agricultural output, including 40 percent of the nation's fruit, 30 percent of its milk, meat, and poultry, and about 60 percent of its potatoes. Of more importance to the Soviet consumer, however, is the fact that the quality of this privately grown produce is vastly superior to that of the produce grown on state farms.

As head of the national agricultural bureaucracy, Gorbachev did much to foster continued high production on the private plots. And, at the same time, he tried to introduce to the state farms incentives similar to those that make the private farmers work with such efficiency and imagination. His endeavors were less than successful, however. The harvests between 1979 and 1982 were either below average or simply disastrous. In uneventful times, such failures might have been catastrophic for Gorbachev's career. But other crises intervened; and instead of finding himself chastised for the poor performance of the agricultural sector, Gorbachev continued his relentless ascent through the ranks of the Party hierarchy.

A map shows the geographical disposition of the main centers of industrial activity in Siberia. It is widely recognized that the future prosperity of the USSR will depend upon whether or not its ongoing program to exploit this singularly inhospitable region's vast natural resources meets its objectives.

5

The Kremlin's Coming Man

On November 17, 1979, Gorbachev was promoted to candidate membership in the Politburo, the elite and restricted group within the central Party apparatus that actually runs the country.

To understand how the Soviet political system works, one must remember that all control rests with the Communist party. In theory, the supreme organ of the Party is the Party congress, but these gatherings are held only once every five years and last for only 10 days or so. Between congresses, power is nominally exercised by the Central Committee, a select group of 300 or so members, who meet twice a year for a few days at a time. Real power, however, rests with two even smaller, more elite groups, the Politburo and the Secretariat of the Central Committee. The Secretariat's task is to monitor the work of the government departments, which are organized in a bureaucracy separate from that of the Party and headed by the Council of Ministers. The chairman of the Council of Ministers is called the prime minister. The Politburo, as its name suggests, is the political bureau of the Central Committee. Its official task is to supervise political

UPI/BETTMANN NEWSPHOTOS

Soviet author Alexander Solzhenitsyn, whose *One Day in the Life of Ivan Denisovich* — a 1962 novel detailing the horrors of Stalin's labor camps — won him universal acclaim. Here the author addresses a Harvard University commencement in 1978, four years after his expulsion from the USSR by the Brezhnev regime, which had taken exception to the antisocialist tenor of his later works.

During the late 1970s, Brezhnev's extreme conservatism became his most pronounced political attribute. The aging leader — and the majority of his cronies — grew increasingly suspicious of the economic experimentation being conducted in Eastern Europe and also became increasingly intolerant of nonconformity inside the USSR.

affairs. In practice, it is the single most powerful body in the country. Moreover, the chairman of the Politburo is normally the Party's general secretary — the most important secretary on the Central Committee. This dual role gives the general secretary precedence over all the other party secretaries and Politburo members. The setup is further complicated by the fact that both the Central Committee and the Politburo have full, or voting, members and candidate, or nonvoting, members. It was to the position of nonvoting member that Gorbachev was appointed in 1979.

Although it might seem that Gorbachev's position in the hierarchy was still relatively low, the reality was not so simple. Membership (even candidate membership) in both the Politburo and the Central Committee Secretariat is enormously prestigious. In addition, the Brezhnev Politburo in the late 1970s was beginning to show its collective age. Brezhnev and his clique had been in their 50s when they ousted Khrushchev, but now their average age was approaching 70. Brezhnev himself had celebrated his 70th birthday in December 1976 and he was obviously not in good health. In fact, all sorts

Soviet Defense Minister Dmitri Ustinov (left) welcomes Cuban Defense Minister Raúl Castro to Moscow on February 21, 1969. Close economic, political, and military ties have existed between the USSR and Cuba since 1961, when Cuban Prime Minister Fidel Castro turned to Moscow for assistance following an abortive invasion of the island by U.S.-backed, anticommunist Cuban exiles.

Soviet physicist Andrei Sakharov (center), who played a prominent part in the development of the first Soviet hydrogen bomb and later became an ardent advocate of nuclear disarmament and a leading dissident, with his wife, Yelena Bonner (second from right), and friends at Moscow's Sheremetyevo Airport, December 20, 1975. Mrs. Bonner was returning from Oslo, Norway, where she had accepted her husband's Nobel Peace Prize, which the Soviet government had refused to allow Sakharov to collect in person.

of rumors were circulating in Moscow concerning his ailments. Even in carefully controlled situations, it was apparent that the elderly general secretary had difficulty moving, speaking, or even concentrating on the issue at hand, let alone remembering what had happened previously. Although Brezhnev and his cronies were not yet prepared to concede power, they had already lost much of the vigor and determination that had enabled them to move up through the Party hierarchy during the Stalin era and reach their present exalted positions. The time was fast approaching when the relative youth and ambition of Gorbachev and his contemporaries would give them distinct political advantages.

Although the Brezhnev generation paid lip service to the need for radical change, especially in the developing nations of Africa and Asia, at home they tended to be extremely conservative. Soviet citizens who urged greater political and intellectual freedom, the so-called dissidents, were subjected to constant harassment by the police and the KGB. Many of them were either imprisoned or kept under house arrest; others were forcibly confined in psychiatric hospitals — on the specious grounds that questioning the system was a sign of mental instability. Brezhnev and his colleagues were also suspicious of economic innovations, especially the kinds of measures that had been adopted in Hungary and Czechoslovakia, where material incentives for industrial and agricultural workers had been intro-

Babrak Karmal, prime minister of the Democratic Republic of Afghanistan and leader of the Soviet-backed ruling party, the People's Democratic party of Afghanistan (PDPA), addresses Afghan students studying at Moscow State University, October 18, 1980. Gorbachev was one of the four Politburo members who ordered the Soviet invasion of Afghanistan in 1979.

duced. Instead, the Brezhnev regime sought to increase output with speeches and newspaper editorials exhorting the workers and officials simply to be more industrous and efficient.

During the Brezhnev era, Party speeches were often aimed at specific targets. For example, Brezhnev himself, in November 1979, referred to the difficulty the central government had encountered in effecting the replacement of inefficient and lazy officials. The general secretary said it was time to "replace those who cannot cope with their assigned work." He even went so far as to name 11 particular officials whose work the Party hierarchy considered inadequate, an action that brought back chilling memories of the Stalinist approach to personnel changes. Such was the state of the Soviet leadership when a major crisis developed in Afghanistan, a small country situated on the Soviet Union's southern border.

Afghanistan has been considered strategically important by Russia's rulers since the days of the tsars. Throughout the 19th century, Afghanistan was the target of Russian and British colonial ambitions in Central Asia. In the early days of Bolshevik and Communist rule, Afghanistan came to be seen as a bulwark for anti-Soviet intervention by Britain and other capitalist powers. In the late 20th century, the political stability and alignment of Afghanistan has been of concern to the governments of the Soviet Union, China, India, Pakistan, and Iran.

The Afghan crisis began in April 1978, when Muhammad Daoud, the man who had ruled Afghanistan since the monarchy was overthrown in 1973, was himself overthrown in a new coup. Daoud had originally been brought to power with Moscow's assistance, but over the years he had turned against the local communists, the People's Democratic party of Afghanistan (PDPA). Finally, even though many of its comrades remained in prison, the PDPA, led by party chief Nur Mohammad Taraki, had struck back. However, Taraki's claim to the leadership was by no means secure. Two of his colleagues, Babrak Karmal and Hafizullah Amin, were also contenders

Opponents of the Soviet-backed communist government of Afghanistan are escorted to prison in October 1980. Since 1979, thousands of Afghan civilians have died in the fighting between antigovernment guerrillas and the Soviet occupation forces.

for command. Following a protracted struggle for power, Karmal emerged as the loser and was exiled to Eastern Europe by Amin. Then, on September 16, 1979, there was yet another coup, in which Taraki was killed and Amin seized power for himself. The situation had become completely unstable. Fighting between various factions — including the rival wings of the PDPA — swept across much of the country. Moscow's erstwhile influence in Afghanistan seemed to have been seriously impaired, and Soviet intelligence officials were claiming that Amin intended to institute a pro-American foreign policy.

The Politburo found itself faced with a number of choices, none of which it considered particularly palatable. Failure to intervene could mean that Afghanistan's internal affairs might become completely chaotic and that the United States or China might move in. The prospect of Chinese or American forces on the Soviet-Afghan border naturally horrified the men in the Kremlin. The Soviet leaders also recognized that the cost of intervention might well outweigh the benefits. From a propaganda point of view, it would be extremely difficult for the Soviet Union to continue to present itself as the champion of revolutions in Africa and Latin America if it crushed one in Afghanistan.

According to authoritative sources, the decision to invade Afghanistan was debated and made by four men: Yuri Andropov, head of the KGB; Foreign Minister Andrei Gromyko; Defense Minister Dmitri Ustinov; and Mikhail Gorbachev. On December 25, 1979, 5,000 Soviet paratroopers stormed the presidential palace in Kabul, the Afghan capital. Two days later, the struggle was over. Amin was dead, and Karmal, the dutiful servant of the Soviet Union, was installed in his place. However, the matter did not end there. Armed resistance to the Soviet-backed Karmal regime continued into the 1980s and tens of thousands of Soviet troops persisted in the struggle against the "counterrevolutionaries."

The manner in which the Soviet leadership reached the decision to invade reveals that major new alignments had developed in the upper reaches of the regime. Brezhnev still retained some of his former importance, but increasingly he was becoming little more than a figurehead. Suslov, though in poor health, had remained a major influence behind the scenes, and is said to have been consulted by telephone during the deliberation on the crisis in Afghanistan. Gromyko, who had previously been known as an executor of other people's decisions, had now advanced to become a decisionmaker in his own right. Ustinov, as defense minister, always had behind him the full political weight of the Soviet military establishment. Gorbachev, who was becoming increasingly close to Andropov, Suslov, and Gromyko, was still something of a junior partner in this formidable coalition, but one with an important power base of his own. As a leading member of the younger generation of Soviet leaders, Gorbachev increasingly came to be seen as a spokesman for that generation. As a former regional party secretary, Gorbachev had come to be regarded as something of a spokesman for that particular stratum of officials as well. Finally, as Central Committee secretary for agriculture, Gorbachev had influence with — and the support of — those who toiled in that vital section of the economy. What opposition there was to Gorbachev's newfound influence would have

Soviet Foreign Minister Andrei Gromyko confers with Indian Prime Minister Indira Gandhi in New Delhi, the Indian capital, on February 12, 1980. Gromyko — whose tendency to develop and pursue foreign-policy initiatives without consulting the Party eventually earned him Gorbachev's disapproval — was briefing Gandhi on the Soviet invasion of Afghanistan.

come from Ustinov and the military-industrial complex whose interests the marshal represented.

The air of crisis engendered by the events in Afghanistan had barely subsided when new tensions arose in another key area where Soviet interests were at stake. Poland, which over the centuries had always resisted Russian domination, was in turmoil again. The communist Polish United Workers party (PZPR), which had been installed as the country's ruling party by the Soviets in 1948, had lost what little support it had ever enjoyed among the Polish people and was riddled with corruption. Moreover, the Roman Catholic church had remained a vital force in Polish society, and was in many ways more potent politically than the PZPR. The election of a Polish churchman — Karol, Cardinal Wojtyla — to the papacy as Pope John Paul II in 1978 had given the Roman Catholic church in Poland increased international visibility at a time when popular dissatisfaction with the government was reaching crisis proportions. Further aggravating the PZPR's predicament was the emergence in the Gdansk shipyards, and later in factories and on farms throughout the entire country, of a new, unofficial trade union called Solidarity. Solidarity sought — in fact, it demanded — a greater measure of democracy in the way the country was run, and an end to the privileges enjoyed, generally undeservedly, by government bureaucrats. As opposition to the regime in Warsaw (the Polish capital) grew into open defiance, it seemed to Gorbachev and his colleagues in the Kremlin that Poland was once again slipping toward social upheavals on the scale of those that had rocked the country in 1956 and 1970.

In September 1980 Edward Gierek, the first secretary of the PZPR, suffered a heart attack and was replaced by Stanislaw Kania, who proved no more capable of containing the situation that had his predecessor. Strikes and work stoppages spread throughout the country, and by the winter of 1980—81, many foreign observers had become convinced that Soviet military intervention in Poland was imminent. For various reasons, not the least of

In September 1981 Wojciech Jaruzelski, Poland's party leader and prime minister, responded to the industrial unrest that had accompanied the emergence of the independent trade union Solidarity by imposing martial law and ordering the union's leaders arrested and sent to prison.

Members of the independent Polish trade union Solidarity demonstrate in Warsaw, the Polish capital, in May 1982. The considerable success of the ruling regime's offensive against Solidarity has virtually paralyzed Poland: millions of that country's citizens have retreated into political apathy.

which was the likelihood that the Poles, communist and noncommunist alike, would unite to resist a Soviet invasion, no military action was taken. Instead, changes were made within the ruling elite in Poland. In February 1981 General Wojciech Jaruzelski, Poland's defense minister, was appointed prime minister, and began to make limited concessions to Solidarity. Eventually, however, Jaruzelski lost patience with both the PZPR — which had failed miserably in its attempts to conciliate the workers — and Solidarity, whose members' industrial actions had virtually crippled the Polish economy. In September 1981 Jaruzelski ousted Kania as the Polish Communist party leader, and immediately began using troops against strikers. In December the Polish authorities, under pressure from the Soviet government, declared martial law throughout the country and arrested many of Solidarity's leaders.

The Brezhnev regime soon discovered that its interventionist policies meant the end of detente. Events in Afghanistan and Poland had made a mockery of the concept of peaceful coexistence. Washington had responded to the invasion of Afghanistan by imposing an embargo on grain shipments to the Soviet Union — a particularly hard blow since the USSR had just suffered another miserable harvest and had also been forced to send grain to Poland, where the political unrest had disrupted that country's agriculture. Then, there was the matter of the 1980 Olympic Games. For the first time in history, the Olympics were to be held in Moscow, and the Soviet government had naturally intended to use the occasion to show Soviet socialism to its best advantage. A vast amount of money had been spent on building new sports facilities and hotels to house the athletes and the thousands of visitors that were expected. However, the United States announced that, in protest against Soviet policy in Afghanistan and Poland, its athletes would not take part in the games. The U.S. government campaigned — successfully — to persuade other nations not to attend. The boycott was deeply resented by the Soviets. Never before had participation in the Olympics been subject to political considerations based on the actions of the host country.

At times during this period the aging Kremlin leadership had seemed unable to cope. Even ordinary Soviet citizens often expressed dissatisfaction with the ineffectiveness they perceived in their leaders. Some concessions had to be made to the march of time, and in October 1980 Aleksei Kosygin finally stepped down as prime minister. Gorbachev was promoted to full membership in the Politburo at

Brezhnev and U.S. President Jimmy Carter sign the SALT II Treaty (which limited certain types of nuclear weapons systems) on June 18, 1979. The spring 1986 announcement by the U.S. government that — due to what it perceived as Soviet violations of the agreements — it would no longer abide by the treaty did little to improve U.S.-Soviet relations.

69

that time. Shortly thereafter, in early 1981, the regime announced more liberal policies on the private plots that supplied the country with so much of its food, and began to discuss possible means of providing greater incentives for those who worked in the state-controlled areas of agriculture.

Despite these limited attempts to pursue more progressive domestic policies, the atmosphere of decadence and decay that seemed to surround the Brezhnev regime could not be dispelled. By the beginning of 1982, rumors that Brezhnev's daughter, Galina Churbanov, was involved in illegal activities were rampant in Moscow. According to one account, the scandal had erupted after the funeral of a former director of the Soviet State Circus, when one of the dead man's friends returned home to discover that she had been robbed of a collection of diamonds. The police later found the jewels in the apartment of a close friend of Galina. This tale served to increase popular dislike of the Brezhnevs, a dislike that was sometimes in evidence in the press. In December 1981, for example, a Leningrad satirical magazine, *Aurora*, devoted an entire issue to the commemoration of Brezhnev's 75th birthday. But shrewd Soviet citizens, used to reading between the lines, were delighted to find that on page 75 was a satirical article about an old man — supposedly a writer — who did not plan to die. The narrator made it clear that he wished the old fellow would die, and voiced extreme disappointment when a report of the writer's death proved false. It was painfully clear that the "writer" was meant to represent the aging Brezhnev.

Normally, such an overt criticism of a senior official could not occur in the Soviet Union unless it had been sanctioned by someone of great political stature. Likewise, the sordid details of the diamond robbery would not usually have become so widely known unless someone with great authority in the KGB or the police had approved the leak. To those familiar with the inner workings of the Soviet system, it seems almost certain that Andropov, or one of his supporters, had a hand in both these instances of political chicanery. Indeed, Andropov was

> *The true leader must submerge himself in the fountain of the people.*
> —VLADIMIR ILICH LENIN

growing ever more prominent. Suslov, the man who had for so long acted as the guardian of Marxist-Leninist orthodoxy, had died in January 1982. Soon after, Andropov had moved from the KGB to the Central Committee Secretariat. He was now ensconced in the significant double role of Central Committee secretary and Politburo member — a combination of positions that has always been an indication of candidacy for supreme power in the Kremlin. As Andropov moved up in the Party hierarchy, Gorbachev, his most favored protegé, moved with him. Andropov, Chernenko, and Gorbachev were now the only three Central Committee secretaries also holding seats on the Politburo.

On November 10, 1982, Leonid Brezhnev died. A few days earlier the old man had appeared in bitterly cold weather to stand on the Lenin Mausoleum in Red Square during celebrations marking the 65th anniversary of the Russian Revolution. Unfortunately, it had been too much for his enfeebled constitution. Even before his funeral, the Central Committee had elected a new general secretary — Yuri Andropov. With this appointment, it seemed that a new era had dawned in the Soviet Union. But nobody could have guessed how brief it would prove to be.

Crowds look on as senior Soviet officials carry Brezhnev's coffin at his funeral in Moscow's Red Square, November 15, 1982. Brezhnev's successor as general secretary of the CPSU was one of Gorbachev's most powerful patrons — Yuri Andropov, formerly head of the KGB (the Soviet secret police) and Central Committee secretary for ideology, international party relations, and foreign policy.

6

Understudy to Andropov

Yuri Andropov was 68 years old when he was elected general secretary, but he appeared to be still in vigorous health. During his first few months in office, Andropov made strenuous efforts to impart a new vigor to the system — efforts that enjoyed considerable popularity among the Soviet people. He traveled to Prague for a meeting of the Warsaw Pact. He warned the Party, even in his first speech as general secretary, that he had no "ready recipes" for economic improvement but that he expected everyone to work harder and more diligently. Andropov even staged "impromptu" visits to factories, such as the Ordzhonikidze machine tool plant in Moscow, to deliver this message to the workers personally.

The appearance of a CPSU general secretary in the workplace was not a new experience for the Soviet people. Several of Andropov's predecessors had paid visits to factories. Khrushchev had positively reveled in touring plants and factories; in the early years of his regime, Brezhnev had also made such visits. Khrushchev and Brezhnev, however, had carefully orchestrated their appearances for pro-

UPI/BETTMANN NEWSPHOTOS

On his December 1984 visit to Great Britain, Gorbachev greatly impressed both the British people and their right-wing, passionately anticommunist prime minister, Margaret Thatcher, who declared: "I like Mr. Gorbachev. We can do business together."

Erich Honecker (left), head of state of the German Democratic Republic, is welcomed to Moscow by CPSU General Secretary Yuri Andropov in May 1983. By this time Andropov's crackdown on drunkenness in the workplace, absenteeism, and poor work performance had begun to convince many Soviet citizens that their government seriously intended to rectify many social problems.

EASTFOTO

paganda purposes; but Andropov's visits had an air of spontaneity and genuine concern for the workers. For the first time in many years, the Soviet people had the feeling that changes for the better might be imminent.

Andropov initiated a new campaign to combat alcoholism, a centuries-old cause of social and economic problems in Russia and the Soviet Union. Official encouragement of abstention from "demon vodka" was frequently combined with a parallel drive to reduce absenteeism. Drunkenness had long been a major cause of lost man-hours in Soviet industry, and the Andropov regime imposed much stiffer penalties for unjustified absence from work. For every day's absence, the offending worker would lose a day's vacation. More importantly, anyone absent for more than three hours in any one day would be docked a whole day's pay. This last rule was important because Soviet workers had often slipped out for several hours at a time to do their shopping while the impossibly long and unavoidable lines were a little shorter.

Andropov's campaign had a spectacular side as well. Special vigilante squads of Party members wearing special red arm bands were assigned to raid cinemas, bathhouses, barbershops and the other places where loafers might have gone instead of going to work. The vigilantes also took to checking the papers of anyone found standing in a store line during normal working hours. Lines did become

Moscow shoppers wait in line at a store that has just received a shipment of shoes, October 1983. Serious shortages of consumer goods — as well as the generally poor quality of such goods — remains a major problem in the USSR, where production, distribution, and pricing are controlled by a central planning bureaucracy rather than by market forces.

UPI/BETTMANN NEWSPHOTOS

Gorbachev and Canadian Federal Agricultural Minister Eugene Whelan examine a glass of wine at an experimental farm near Ottawa, the Canadian capital, on May 19, 1983. During his visit to Canada, Gorbachev showed a special interest in touring farms and factories and meeting ordinary working people.

noticeably shorter, but this was partly because Andropov had arranged for some of the larger factories to open their own shoe repair and dry cleaning facilities to help workers avoid the need to cut into work time to accomplish their daily chores.

Andropov also replaced the leader of the domestic police, and called on them to put an end to corruption, which had become a serious concern. Politburo meetings were finally reported in the newspapers, although the reports still did not reveal much of what actually transpired. Local and regional Party organizations were instructed to stage special meetings for "accounting and election," in which members would have to present and defend their accomplishments. People began to think that a wholesale revamping of the Party leadership was planned.

In typical Russian fashion, this rash of activity gave birth to a whole new series of cynical jokes. For example: A Soviet chicken tells a friend that she is puzzled by the new turn in official requirements. Under Lenin, she tells the friend, she was required to lay dozens of eggs. Under Stalin, life became so full of terror and hardship that she could lay only a few eggs. Output declined still further under Khrushchev, who told her to fly to the moon. Under Brezhnev, the situation became so confused that she took to drink. And then Andropov takes over and tells her that the most important thing she can do is get to work on time!

Despite the cynicism with which his initiatives

were often received, Andropov did succeed in creating a new atmosphere. It was readily apparent to the Soviet people that a strong man had taken charge. Andropov's obvious intention to promote new, younger, and, therefore, more vigorous officials furthered this image. The tough Leningrad Party leader, Grigori Romanov, who had been a full Politburo member since 1976, was brought to Moscow to work as a Central Committee secretary. Again, these dual positions put Romanov in a strong position to succeed Andropov as general secretary. Nikolai Ryzhkov, an engineer who had won a reputation as a particularly efficient industrial manager, was also promoted to the Central Committee Secretariat. At the time, Ryzhkov's promotion was considered just one of several similar changes in the Secretariat, but later it acquired greater significance. Gorbachev, in his role as the man trying to rejuvenate the leadership, may well have inspired this move. Geidar Aliyev, a former chief of the KGB in the Azerbaijani Soviet Socialist Republic and later the Party leader there, was also brought to Moscow as a Central Committee secretary at this time.

Gorbachev was given the task of supervising the changes in the regional and local Party organizations. Considering the entrenched interests of the current officeholders, Gorbachev faced an extremely difficult task, one full of the risks that any such sweeping transition can generate. But, on the other hand, Gorbachev would then enjoy the support of the new officeholders, since they would owe their jobs to his intervention. In just such a way had major power bases been built in the past in the Soviet Union. Gorbachev also retained his position as Central Committee secretary for agriculture. Andropov seems to have given him more or less a free hand in determining the proper policies even though the only result was a succession of disastrous harvests.

Andropov also had to be cautious about making changes. Some of the older officials were permitted to retain their titles, even though it was quite apparent that the bulk of their duties had been assumed by younger men. In some cases, this was

Soviet citizens have the right to criticize and to make proposals. But it is an entirely different matter when a few individuals transform criticism into anti-Soviet activity, violate the law, supply Western propaganda centers with false information, disseminate false rumors, try to organize anti-social actions.

—YURI ANDROPOV
Soviet leader

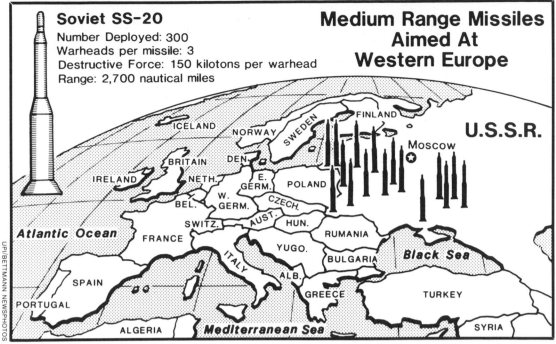

Soviet SS-20
Number Deployed: 300
Warheads per missile: 3
Destructive Force: 150 kilotons per warhead
Range: 2,700 nautical miles

Medium Range Missiles Aimed At Western Europe

seen as a gesture to the remnants of what might be called the Brezhnev faction, people who had been close to the former leader, but this was not always the case. Konstantin Chernenko, for example, had often been regarded as one of Brezhnev's closest associates. Their friendship dated back to their service together in the Moldavian Soviet Socialist Republic during the Stalin era. In fact, there had been wide speculation that Chernenko was Brezhnev's own choice as his successor. In accordance with this belief, it was frequently suggested that as part of the political maneuvering that had brought Andropov to power, a deal had been struck whereby Chernenko would later be named chairman, or president, of the Supreme Soviet — the official head of state. Brezhnev had been both general secretary and head of state. After his death, the presidency had been left vacant. Then, in June 1983, Andropov was elected president and, significantly, he was nominated for the position by Chernenko. And as Chernenko's star seemed to fade, Gorbachev's shone ever brighter.

For a relatively new member of the ruling elite, Gorbachev was accorded unusual prominence in several ways. In 1983 he was chosen to lead an official delegation to Canada. The choice of Canada

In March 1982 the Soviet government announced that it had decided to freeze at existing levels the number of medium-range, triple-warhead SS-20 nuclear missiles stationed in the western USSR. The subsequent American deployment of single-warhead Pershing II and ground-launched cruise missiles in Western Europe to counter the threat posed by the Soviet SS-20s was still in progress in 1986.

was certainly no accident. The Soviet Union and Canada are similar in many ways: geographically, they both occupy huge land masses; and although a full 270 million people live in the Soviet Union, both countries are relatively thinly populated; furthermore, as a result of immigration patterns to Canada, even the population makeup is very similar. A sizable proportion of the inhabitants of the Canadian prairies is of Ukrainian, Russian, Polish, or other Slavic descent. Moreover, over the years Canada has proved a reliable trading partner to the Soviet Union, as a supplier of grain, for instance, when the United States either would not or could not do so. Finally, since the days of Stalin, Canada has been used by Moscow as a sort of testing ground for dealing with the United States. To the Soviets there is little difference between the respective natures of these two North American nations.

Gorbachev arrived in Ottawa, the Canadian capital, in May 1983. He had been abroad several times before, of course, but this trip was different. This time, Gorbachev was traveling as one of the most important men in the Soviet Union, and his every move would be watched. Observers were in for some interesting surprises. While in the Canadian capital, Gorbachev appeared before a session of a Canadian parliamentary committee on foreign and defense affairs. No one could recall such a high-ranking Soviet official ever having made such an appearance. Since many members of the committee were of Russian or other Eastern European descent, an interesting debate was expected.

Gorbachev, putting on a flashy performance, did not disappoint them. He was charming, intelligent, well-informed, authoritative, and witty. But, at the same time, he showed that he could be tough, even rude, and he was able to score some propaganda points with his ability to turn a thorny question into an accusation of the questioner. For example, in reply to a question about the state of affairs in Poland, he said: "We are not indifferent to what is taking place in a fraternal country, and during this period of internal processes and changes in Poland, the Western countries have taken the position of an

These people are given advice and explanations to help them to understand reality. If they persist in their actions and continue to be so-called "dissidents" and even violate the law, we treat them quite differently. They must be punished with the full force of Soviet law.

—YURI ANDROPOV
Soviet leader

economic blockade of Poland, and have in point of fact compromised the economic relations established with the country. They have deprived the country itself and its enterprises of the opportunity to operate and function normally." But he could be conciliatory, too. "We in the Soviet Union," he said, "are sure that the 1970s, which were years of detente, were not an accidental episode in the difficult history of mankind. The policy of detente has not run its course. The term detente has taken a firm place in the political dictionary because the future belongs to detente." And then he added, "Not confrontation, but mutually advantageous collaboration — that is our program."

After leaving Ottawa, Gorbachev was taken on a guided tour of the farming and industrial areas of Ontario. He visited Toronto and, like any other tourist, was taken to see the famous Niagara Falls. But what interested him the most, it seemed, was the opportunity to visit Canadian factories and farms and to talk to the workers about what made them so much more productive than their counterparts in the Soviet Union. One of the places he visited, for example, was the Heinz ketchup factory in Leamington, Ontario. He questioned the workers there about whether or not they worked overtime, about whether or not they owned more than one car or a second home, about whether their children were going to college, and so on. It was like Andropov at the Ordzhonikidze machine tool works all over again.

After a few days touring southern Ontario, Gorbachev and his party moved on to Alberta, where they were to inspect new methods of farming drylands similar to the many areas of the Soviet Union where rainfall is irregular. However, the group had just reached western Canada when Gorbachev an-

A cruise missile rises from its launcher at a testing site in the United States. The U.S. and its allies' deployment of such systems in Western Europe has greatly angered the Soviets, who consider the cruise missile a first-strike weapon.

On an invitation from the Soviet government, Samantha Smith, an American schoolgirl from Maine, tours Red Square, Moscow, with her parents in July 1983. Samantha's letter to Soviet Premier Andropov expressing her fervent wish for world peace struck a responsive chord in both Americans and Russians.

nounced that, for unexpected reasons, it was necessary for him to return immediately to the Soviet Union. The Russians were close-mouthed about the exact reason for Gorbachev's abrupt departure, but from subsequent statements it is now reasonably certain that it was at this time that Andropov had become seriously ill.

Once back in Moscow, Gorbachev was given an increasingly public role as one of the main figures of the regime. But that prominence was offset by the emergence of Romanov as a possible successor to Andropov. It was quickly noted that Gorbachev seemed to have developed a friendly relationship with Romanov, who had over the years earned a reputation as a prickly customer. On one occasion during this period, during a meeting of the Supreme Soviet, the two were seated on the platform while Andrei Gromyko was speaking. Since the speech was televised, Soviet viewers were able to see that during Gromyko's address Gorbachev and Romanov were conducting a lively and affable exchange behind his back. First Gorbachev would say something; then Romanov would answer. Their smiles were frequent.

Andropov was now making few public appearances and would often disappear from view for weeks at a time. Stories began to circulate that he was suffering from severe kidney disease. According to reliable accounts that emerged later, Andropov was using Gorbachev as the unofficial and exclusive executor of his wishes. Gorbachev would visit the ailing general secretary at the secluded clinic outside Moscow where he was being treated, get his instructions, and convey them to the rest of the leadership. Publicly, Gorbachev was also being used as a stand-in for Andropov. For example, in July 1983, when government delegations from Hungary and West Germany visited Moscow, Gorbachev was their principal host, though the obviously enfeebled Andropov did manage to put in an appearance.

In October 1983 Gorbachev was chosen to lead yet another foreign mission. This time he was sent to Portugal. In the theater of European politics and economic affairs, Portugal is hardly a major actor, but, from Moscow's point of view, the meeting of the Portuguese Communist party would provide a useful platform not only for sending a message to the other communist parties of Western Europe, but to the region's noncommunist politicians as well. The Kremlin wished to convey its concern over the defense policies being followed by the Reagan administration in the United States, especially the president's plan to conduct research on the Strategic Defense Initative, or "Star Wars," missile defense system in space. In a speech that he delivered in Lisbon, the Portuguese capital, Gorbachev as-

We must be ready to employ trickery, deceit, law-breaking, withholding and concealing truth. We can and must write in the language which sows among the masses hate, revulsion, scorn and the like, toward those who disagree with us.
—VLADIMIR ILICH LENIN

On September 7, 1983, Korean residents in Japan protest outside the Soviet Embassy in Tokyo seven days after a Korean Airlines Boeing 747 that strayed into Soviet airspace was shot down by a Soviet fighter. The downing of the South Korean airliner caused the Soviet government immense embarrassment and severely damaged East-West relations.

serted: "The essence of the present militaristic course of the U.S.A. is to ensure for itself a dominant position in the world, without ensuring the rights and interests of other states and peoples. For this reason the military potential of the U.S.A. is being strengthened, and the large-scale programs of production of newer and newer types of weapons, the militarization of the oceans and of outer space, are being realized." This combative statement was largely overlooked at the time, but it was probably a true reflection of Gorbachev's views, and was echoed later when he and U.S. President Ronald Reagan finally met.

Relations between the United States and the Soviet Union had reached a low point during this period. The policy of detente, which Brezhnev had done so much to foster, had fallen by the wayside after the election of Ronald Reagan, who was much more hostile toward the Soviets than his three immediate predecessors — Presidents Jimmy Carter, Gerald Ford, and Richard Nixon. The hostile state of affairs was vividly illustrated in the late summer by a tragic incident in the Far East.

On September 1, 1983, a Korean Airlines Boeing 747 airliner bound for Seoul, the South Korean capital, took off from Anchorage, Alaska, with 269 people aboard. En route, the plane veered off the normal flight path — for reasons that will probably never be discovered — and began to fly over Soviet territory. The Soviet government, at least as much as any other, is sensitive to such incursions into its air space; and in the Far East there are also many key military bases. So when the Korean airliner overflew what the Soviet authorities later said were important military installations on the Kamchatka Peninsula and on the island of Sakhalin, Soviet fighter planes were sent up in pursuit. Apparently, the Korean pilot either could not or would not answer calls to land, and the plane was shot down by missiles fired by the Soviet fighters. Everyone on board the plane was killed.

Public opinion in the West was outraged by what seemed to be the deliberate destruction of a commercial airliner and the deliberate killing of the civilians on board. The strong reaction obviously surprised and discomfited Soviet authorities. There was some confusion, at first, in the way that they handled the crisis. Marshal Nikolai Ogarkov, at the time one of the highest-ranking military figures in the country, was presented at a highly unusual press conference to offer Moscow's version of what had happened. The Soviets justified themselves by contending that the plane had actually been on a spy mission for the Central Intelligence Agency — though why Washington would want to risk the lives of so many innocent people on a mission that could have been more easily achieved using satellites and military aircraft was never explained. Perhaps the most notable aspect of the whole episode was that, for the most part, the civilian leadership of the Soviet Union was in the background during the worst days of the crisis. To some observers this seemed to suggest that, contrary to previous experience and politics, the decision to shoot down the airliner had been undertaken by the military command, without the approval of the political leadership. This sus-

Vitali Vorotnikov, prime minister of the Russian Soviet Federated Socialist Republic, became a full member of the Politburo in December 1983. Vorotnikov is one of Gorbachev's closest political allies, and has proven a zealous opponent of corruption.

picion was reinforced when Marshal Nikolai Ogarkov, who up to that time had been one of the leading figures in the regime, was dismissed from his position as chief of the general staff of the Soviet armed forces.

The outcome of the Korean Airlines tragedy was that relations between Moscow and Washington, which had seemed to be warming following the August signing of a new grain sales agreement between the United States and the Soviet Union, had once again become antagonistic.

Nevertheless, Andropov — often through Gorbachev — continued to speak hopefully of improving relations. Early in December 1983, Gorbachev met a banker from Coon Rapids, Iowa, in the Kremlin. The meeting was inspired by a letter from an Iowa newspaper editor to Andropov. The editor recalled that in 1959 Nikita Khrushchev had paid a visit to Iowa that had helped to ease tensions and promote better understanding between the American and Soviet peoples. Andropov, through Gorbachev, passed on the word that he too was concerned about the tensions that had developed. But Gorbachev made it only too clear that the Soviets considered Washington entirely responsible for the deterioration in U.S.-Soviet relations. It was a very brief meeting, and Andropov's failure to attend served to reinforce the widespread belief that he was gravely ill. This feeling had grown since early November, when the general secretary had failed to make what had previously been a mandatory appearance in Red Square, for the parade and ceremony marking the anniversary of the Russian Revolution.

Nevertheless, Andropov's protegés continued to be promoted within the regime. Most notable was the appointment of Vitali Vorotnikov to be a full member of the Politburo. Other younger men, known for their allegiance to Andropov, were also brought to new prominence at a Central Committee meeting in December 1983. Again, Andropov was absent, but a message from him was read to the assembly. Despite the general secretary's absence, sweeping changes continued to be carried out

> *In the end, one or the other will triumph—a funeral dirge will be sung over the Soviet Republic, or over world capitalism.*
>
> —VLADIMIR ILICH LENIN

within the Party leadership, especially at the regional level. Gorbachev played a key role in the selection of these new officials. By February 1984, it was reported that he had helped replace 19 of the 150 regional Party secretaries. Fifteen others, of similar rank, had been ousted earlier. Many of the newcomers, like Gorbachev, had emerged from the Komsomol into full-time Party positions. Gorbachev's role in the changes could be clearly detected in events such as the election of a new Party secretary in Leningrad.

It might have been expected, given Romanov's long tenure in Leningrad, that he would naturally be the one chosen to represent the central leadership at the election of the Party chief in the country's second most important city. Instead, it was Gorbachev who arrived in the former capital to nominate the new secretary. Observers in the Soviet Union and abroad took careful note that Gorbachev was accorded VIP treatment, including a visit to the old cruiser *Aurora*, a floating museum that is an important symbol of the revolution.

Suddenly, but not unexpectedly, a two-paragraph statement broadcast on Soviet radio and television at 2:30 P.M. Moscow time on February 10, 1984, announced that Andropov had died the previous day "after a long illness . . . complicated by a chronic kidney deficiency."

Senior Soviet officials escort Andropov's coffin at his funeral in Moscow's Red Square, February 14, 1984. Andropov, who died of kidney disease on February 9, 1984, was succeeded as CPSU general secretary by Konstantin U. Chernenko (at head of column of mourners at right), a leading member of the Brezhnevite faction within the party.

7

Waiting and Consolidating

Andropov's death, after only 14 months in office, was in many ways a great disappointment to the Soviet people. The vigor with which the new general secretary had sought to lift the country out of its lethargy during his first brief months of activity had touched a popular chord. Suddenly, everything seemed doomed to slip back into the old rut. This feeling was reinforced when, after some hesitation, the name of the new general secretary was announced — 72-year-old Konstantin Chernenko.

Chernenko's election to the highest office in the Soviet Union has often been attributed to his close connections with Brezhnev. The two had worked together for many years in the Moldavian Soviet Socialist Republic. Chernenko had been born into a peasant family in Siberia in 1911, and as a young man had held various Party posts in the Krasnoyarsk region. In 1948 he was moved to Moldavia, where Brezhnev was appointed Party leader only two years later. After Brezhnev was moved to Moscow in the last years of the Stalin era and named a Party secretary in 1956, Chernenko followed. From then on, Chernenko continued to move up the ladder just

TASS FROM SOVFOTO

A Soviet scientist (at center of group, wearing suit and tie) instructs students from Algeria, Afghanistan, Iraq, and Angola — all of whose governments have close political, economic, and military ties with the USSR — in petrochemical engineering at an oil rig near Baku, the capital of the Azerbaijan Soviet Socialist Republic.

A prominent Brezhnevite who enjoyed the support of both the Soviet foreign-policy establishment and the nation's military and industrial chief, Konstantin U. Chernenko was appointed general secretary of the CPSU on February 13, 1984. Chernenko, an uninspired and unimaginative politician, had few allies within the ranks of the younger generation of Soviet leaders.

TASS FROM SOVFOTO

a rung behind his friend. Now Brezhnev was dead, and Chernenko ruled in his place.

It soon became apparent, however, that Chernenko, too, was in poor health, and that his tenure as general secretary was certain to be brief. Once again, the Soviet political apparatus would be forced to just sit and mark time. Or would it? Not if Gorbachev and his younger colleagues could help it.

As Chernenko's influence seemed to wane, that of Gorbachev was on the rise. Soon he was being referred to by other senior Soviet officials as the "second general secretary," which implied that Gorbachev held as much power as Chernenko. Stories began to circulate in Moscow that Chernenko had to be carried by aides to a performance at the Bolshoi Theater. Other stories had him being treated at a Moscow clinic for high Party officials. In the general secretary's absence, Gorbachev was said to be acting as chairman of the Politburo.

But to the surprise of many, in April 1984 Chernenko was still sufficiently well to appear at a session of the Supreme Soviet, where he was elected to the presidency of the Soviet Union. The man who nominated Chernenko for the post was none other than Gorbachev, who was himself elected chairman of the foreign affairs commission of the Council of the Union (one of the two chambers of the Supreme Soviet). It was quickly noted by astute observers that Chernenko had previously held the chairmanship of that commission, which had earlier been held for decades by Suslov. Gorbachev was also appointed to govern in yet another longtime Suslov department, that which supervised the work of the Central Committee Secretariat. These two functions, as the leading figure concerned with foreign policy and as the principal supervisor of the Party bureaucracy, would soon be publicly displayed.

In June 1984 Gorbachev was delegated to represent the Soviet Union at the funeral of Enrico Berlinguer, longtime leader of the Italian Communist party (PCI). Like the earlier visit to Portugal, the trip would be an opportunity for Gorbachev to make an on-the-spot assessment of the less Moscow-centered brand of communism called Eurocommunism, of which Berlinguer had been an early and prominent advocate. Gorbachev was also the most prominent official patron during the summer Friendship Games in Moscow, which had been organized after the Soviet Union decided to boycott the Olympic Games in Los Angeles.

In September 1984 Gorbachev appeared in yet another leading role. The episode began when several of the Eastern European communist nations began to show signs of mending their relationships with West Germany. Apparently Chancellor Helmut Kohl of West Germany and the East German leader, Erich Honecker, had held brief discussions on improving and increasing ties between their two nations while they were in Moscow to attend Andropov's funeral. Part of the plan was to have Honecker visit the West German capital, Bonn. He would be the first East German leader to make such a journey. Shortly thereafter, Nicolae Ceauşescu, leader of the Romanian Communist party, and Todor Zhivkov, leader

Soviet and Cuban students in Moscow participate in a street-cleaning campaign in April 1979. Providing education for students from foreign countries dependent on Soviet support has long been an integral element of the Soviet government's endeavors to increase its influence abroad.

Gorbachev and British Prime Minister Margaret Thatcher pose for the press in London in December 1984. In one of the several conciliatory speeches that he delivered during his visit, Gorbachev declared: "For all that separates us, we have one planet, and Europe is our common home, not a theater of operations."

UPI/BETTMANN NEWSPHOTOS

of the Bulgarian Communist party, were reported to have decided to follow Honecker's example. When Ceauşescu, who had long been something of a maverick in the Communist world, decided to go to Bonn, it probably did not cause particularly great concern in Moscow. But when Zhivkov, who is generally regarded as Moscow's most obedient ally, announced plans for a trip to the West German capital, the men in the Kremlin swung into action. First, a heavy propaganda campaign attacking West Germany's involvement in the defensive alliance known as the North Atlantic Treaty Organization was initiated. NATO's plans to deploy new missiles in Western Europe were heavily criticized. Honecker obviously got the message. In early September, he canceled his visit to Bonn. But Zhivkov, of all people, seemed to be intent on going through with his plans. On September 8, 1984, Mikhail Gorbachev arrived in Sofia, the Bulgarian capital. Officially, he was there to help mark the 40th anniversary of communist rule in Bulgaria. But by the time he left, Zhivkov had canceled his proposed visit to Bonn.

Two months later, Gorbachev was himself off on another highly publicized journey to the West. From the time he arrived in Great Britain in mid-December 1984, Gorbachev became the man of the hour.

The British press was quickly captivated by the forthright style of the man who by now was generally regarded as the heir-apparent in the Kremlin. They were equally impressed by Raisa Gorbachev's sophistication. The fact that Raisa could speak English, even hesitantly, made her seem all the more unusual.

As he had done in Canada, Gorbachev agreed to appear before a parliamentary committee. Once again it was a magnificent performance. Gorbachev managed to get across the points that the Soviet media had been making in attacking the military plans of the Reagan administration, while at the same time expressing the Soviet government's desire for the revival of detente. "We still believe," he said, "that there is and can be no rational alternative to the policy of peaceful coexistence, and I would like to emphasize this point with all certainty." Upon further elaboration, he struck a theme that

I left Moscow on March 3, seven days before Konstantin Chernenko's death. The mood was one of gloom, frustration, impatience and embarrassment—gloom about the country's huge problems, frustration with the inactivity of those who were supposed to lead, impatience with an "old guard" of party leaders who refused to yield power and embarrassment that a great nation and great power was essentially leaderless.
—SEWERYN BIALER
American expert on
Soviet affairs

TASS FROM SOVFOTO

Soviet athletes parade in Moscow's V. I. Lenin Stadium on August 18, 1984, at the commencement of the Friendship Games, which were organized by the Soviet government following its decision to boycott the 1984 Summer Olympics in Los Angeles. Gorbachev was the most prominent official patron of the Friendship Games.

found a ready audience in London. "We all agree," he said, "that ours is a vulnerable, fragile yet interdependent world where we must coexist, whether we want this or not. For all that separates us, we have one planet, and Europe is our common home, not a theater of operations."

But perhaps the most striking aspect of the visit came following the talks that Gorbachev had with Prime Minister Margaret Thatcher. Thatcher was clearly most impressed. "I like Mr. Gorbachev," she said. "We can do business together." Coming from a woman who had made a whole political career out of opposing socialism and communism, this was unusual praise indeed.

Suddenly, again as in Canada, the visit to Britain was cut short because of events in Moscow. As Gorbachev explained to a surprised audience of report-

Gorbachev meets with his constituents in Moscow on February 20, 1985, shortly before he was reelected to the USSR Supreme Soviet, the Soviet parliament.

Gorbachev (front row, second from right) and other senior Soviet officials attend a gala performance at Moscow's Bolshoi Theater on March 7, 1985, just three days before CPSU General Secretary Chernenko died, at age 73, of emphysema.

ers in Edinburgh, Scotland, there had been another death in the Soviet leadership — that of Defense Minister Ustinov. So Gorbachev hurried home for yet another Red Square funeral.

As the grey Russian winter of 1984 deepened, the Soviet people sensed that other important funerals were imminent. Rumors of Chernenko's poor health abounded. A Warsaw Pact meeting was canceled, reportedly because the general secretary was too ill to attend. Greek Prime Minister Andreas Papandreou came to Moscow in February 1985, but, contrary to what might have been expected for a visiting leader whom Moscow had been at such pains to court in the past, he never met with Chernenko, which added even greater credibility to the growing suspicions.

Then, in March 1985, Soviet radio and television stations began once again to broadcast the solemn music that precedes all announcements of the death of a Soviet leader. After just 13 months as general secretary, Konstantin Chernenko was dead.

8

The Man in Charge

On March 13, 1985, crowds gathered in Red Square for the third time in 17 months to witness the funeral of a general secretary of the CPSU. Once again, Soviet television carried the ceremony live. This time, however, a different attitude on the part of both the people and the leadership could be discerned. Although Chernenko was accorded due ceremony as a deceased head of state, it was apparent to Western observers that the Soviets were treating the ritual as little more than a formality.

In contrast to the hesitancy that had characterized the Central Committee's deliberations concerning the election of a successor to Andropov, a certain eagerness to arrive at a decision quickly pervaded the power-broking that led to Gorbachev's election. At the Politburo meeting that took place just three hours after Chernenko died, Gorbachev's leading rival, Grigori Romanov, proposed Moscow Party chief Viktor Grishin for the position of general secretary. When Gorbachev backer Andrei Gromyko, the foreign minister, then hit back by reminding the assembled members of the 70-year-old Grishin's failure to tackle corruption in Moscow, and pointed

Gorbachev's daughter, Irina, and granddaughter, Oksana, attend the traditional May Day celebrations in Moscow in 1985.

Gorbachev delivers the closing speech at the Twenty-Seventh Congress of the CPSU, March 6, 1986. During his address, Gorbachev emphasized the importance of modernizing the nation's industry and agriculture, and declared that this would be done in strict accordance with the principles of scientific socialism.

TASS FROM SOVFOTO

REUTERS/BETTMANN NEWSPHOTOS

out that the Soviet Union needed a general secretary who would live to lead it into the 21st century, the Politburo decided in favor of Gorbachev.

When the Central Committee met on the following day, Gromyko, who had now emerged as Gorbachev's most powerful supporter, discovered that a substantial proportion of its members were not convinced that Gorbachev was the man for the job. Gromyko then delivered a speech of proposal that was not reported in the Soviet press for the simple reason that it was not so much a formal address as a violent tirade. The veteran diplomat's hard-hitting performance had the desired effect, however, and Gorbachev became general secretary.

From the moment he came to power, Gorbachev made it clear that he was impatient to get the Soviet economy moving. In his acceptance speech he said bluntly: "We are to achieve a decisive turn in transferring the national economy to the tracks of intensive development. We should, we are bound to attain within the briefest period the most advanced scientific and technical positions, the highest world level in the productivity of social labor."

The complete overhaul of the Party machinery and the government bureaucracy that Gorbachev had begun during Andropov's incumbency was now accelerated. There was considerable resistance to this development among the older, firmly entrenched officials, but among their younger colleagues and the

Gorbachev and French President François Mitterrand conduct a press conference in Paris in October 1985. During his visit to France, Gorbachev consistently expressed his desire for rapprochement between East and West, and voiced his conviction that the United States and the USSR should reach broad agreement on how best to preserve world peace.

REUTERS/BETTMANN NEWSPHOTOS

people at large there was a genuine feeling that a major campaign to rejuvenate the system was long overdue. That Gorbachev and his followers had no desire to give the Soviet people the impression that the task would be easy was apparent from the cautionary note sounded in official statements. An editorial in *Izvestia* declared, "We have had two decades of inertia, and it is going to take time to get the country moving again."

Some of Gorbachev's other measures also seemed to have their roots in policies implemented during the Andropov era. The crackdown on absenteeism, laziness, and corruption in the workplace was intensified. Those who violated the strict new regulations were fined; if they failed to reform, they were dismissed. Pilfering from the workplace and other minor misdemeanors that had often been overlooked in the past now brought stiff jail sentences.

Gorbachev recognized that it would be impossible to motivate the workers by coercion alone. Accordingly, new incentives were offered to industrial and agricultural workers to increase production. Changing the workers' entrenched cynicism — which is perfectly expressed in one of their favorite maxims: "They pretend to pay us and we pretend to work" — would not be easy, but Gorbachev was determined to try.

When Gorbachev took over as general secretary, he introduced on a much wider scale experiments originally launched early in the 1980s whereby plant managers were allowed more authority to decide what and how much their factories would produce. (Previously, such decisions had almost invariably been made by Gosplan — the State Planning Commission — in Moscow.) Another revolutionary innovation that Gorbachev ordered retained was the rewarding of those responsible for increased production and efficiency with higher pay.

Gorbachev was also determined to scrap the practice of rating factories and their managers purely in terms of the quantity of goods produced. In the past, all a factory had to do to secure official approval was to meet or exceed its quota. Neither the planners nor the managers were much concerned with prod-

> *The whole economic strategy being pursued by the new leadership probably appears radical to many Soviet citizens, including many senior officials.*
> —PHILIP HANSON
> British specialist on the
> Soviet economy

uct quality. Now factors such as promptness of delivery, product quality, and even consumer demand were to be taken into account. Similar experiments were being conducted throughout the agricultural sector. The collective farms now had more autonomy in deciding what to grow and where to sell it.

Gorbachev's commitment to expanding the production of consumer goods was very much in evidence when he visited Leningrad in May 1985. He avoided the city's heavy industrial complexes and made well-publicized tours of an electrical appliance plant and a clothing factory. In a speech that he made during the Leningrad visit, Gorbachev declared, "All Leningrad products should be of world-market standard — no less!"

The most sweeping changes that Gorbachev undertook were those in the Party and government apparatus. Among these changes, Romanov, once considered Gorbachev's main rival for the leadership, was "retired" from the Politburo, on July 1, 1985, ostensibly for health reasons, but actually because Gorbachev regarded Romanov's Brezhnevite conservatism as a political liability. During his time in Leningrad, Romanov had concentrated on beefing up heavy industry and had never shown any interest in advanced technology. He was an ardent advocate of central planning and had a pathological hatred of all things Western.

Following Romanov's dismissal, Lev Zaikov, who had succeeded him as Leningrad Party chief, was promoted to full Politburo membership. A former manager of a military plant, Zaikov shares Gorbachev's enthusiasm for advanced technology.

On July 2, 1985, the 1,500 delegates to the Supreme Soviet — the Soviet parliament — witnessed what was perhaps the most surprising of Gorbachev's changes in government and Party personnel. Gorbachev proposed that Gromyko should be elected chairman of the Presidium of the Supreme Soviet — thus becoming Soviet head of state — and relieved of his duties as foreign minister and first deputy prime minister. That Gromyko was not exactly overjoyed at his election to this prestigious but largely ceremonial position was evident from the

Sounding at times more like an evangelical preacher than a communist leader, he has campaigned against corruption and alcoholism, exhorted workers to double their efforts, abolished government agencies, dismissed scores of senior managers and talked bluntly about economic failings.
—*The New York Times,*
February 23, 1986

complete lack of emotion that he displayed while delivering his acceptance speech.

What happened next seemed even more incredible to the delegates. Prime Minister Nikolai Tikhonov stepped forward and proposed that Eduard Shevardnadze, Party leader of the Georgian Soviet Socialist Republic, succeed Gromyko as foreign minister. The delegates found it hard to believe that a provincial Party leader with no experience of foreign affairs was being proposed as a successor to the world's longest-serving foreign minister.

Securing Shevardnadze's election as foreign minister was actually one of Gorbachev's most brilliant moves. With one stroke, he had removed the foreign ministry from the hands of a career diplomat and brought it back under direct Party control. His selection of a man without foreign experience also meant that he himself would assume responsibility for foreign policy. He would propound the Party line on foreign policy and Shevardnadze would simply follow it.

The next major change came when Tikhonov, who had had his draft of a Five Year Plan thrown back at him by Gorbachev for reworking in the summer of 1985, was retired on September 25, 1985. His successor was 55-year-old Nikolai Ryzhkov, formerly first deputy chairman of Gosplan and, under An-

Soviet Foreign Minister Eduard A. Shevardnadze confers with U.S. Secretary of State George Shultz in New York on September 25, 1985. Formerly Party leader of the Georgian Soviet Socialist Republic, Shevardnadze, who is one of Gorbachev's most loyal supporters, was appointed foreign minister in July 1985.

dropov, the architect of a new Central Committee coordination department designed to ensure more efficient management of industry and reductions in the size of the Gosplan bureaucracy. On October 14, 1985, Nikolai Baibakov, for 20 years the head of Gosplan, was dismissed, reportedly because he opposed Gorbachev's proposals to decentralize some of the economic decision-making.

The major personnel changes effected by Gorbachev added yet another scathingly cynical political joke to the thousands that are constantly in circulation in Soviet society: "Who supports Gorbachev in the Politburo?" it was asked. "No one. He's still young enough to stand on his own." Gorbachev's youthful vigor certainly stood in great contrast to the infirmity (and, in the case of Chernenko and Brezhnev, the near-senility) of the last three of his predecessors.

The changes made by Gorbachev at the less exalted levels of the Soviet hierarchy were also dramatic. Three new secretaries and seven new heads of department have been added to the Central Committee. Within just months of taking office, Gorbachev had supervised the replacement of nearly half of the roughly 100 regional secretaries who formed the single largest and most influential bloc in the 319-member committee.

For the average Soviet citizen, the most obvious innovation made by Gorbachev concerned vodka. In a highly publicized campaign to combat alcoholism, more than two-thirds of the country's liquor stores were closed. Hours of sale in liquor stores and hours

> *It is important to conduct all management and education so that life itself is severe on those who would like to live better and work less.*
>
> —MIKHAIL GORBACHEV

Raisa Gorbachev and Nancy Reagan, wife of U.S. President Ronald Reagan, attend the unveiling of the cornerstone for a new museum at the headquarters of the International Committee of the Red Cross on November 20, 1985, in Geneva, Switzerland, where their husbands were conducting a summit meeting.

REUTERS/BETTMANN NEWSPHOTOS

when liquor could be served in restaurants and elsewhere were sharply curtailed. Heavy restrictions were imposed on the production of wine, brandy, and vodka. Fines for public drunkenness were increased tenfold.

Although it is not often officially admitted, the abuse of alcohol has long been a problem in the Soviet Union. Since the days of the tsars, Western visitors have continually expressed amazement at the sheer quantity of vodka consumed by the average Russian. The toll in broken homes, battered wives, malformed children, and ruined careers has often aroused public distress and official exasperation. Gorbachev's campaign aimed to put an end to this desperate situation and to bring about a fundamental change in Soviet social behavior. There was much grumbling, but within a few months most Soviet citizens seemed to have adjusted. And Western visitors, previously accustomed to having lunches drowned in vodka strongly urged upon them by their exuberant Soviet hosts, now found their official hosts serving lemonade and mineral water instead.

> *How could someone so nice and human run the Soviet system?*
> —DENIS HEALEY
> British statesman

Gorbachev was very much aware of the importance of public relations. Even while Chernenko was still alive, Gorbachev and his family gained much public attention when he, Raisa, their daughter Irina, and granddaughter Oksana arrived at a Moscow polling station to cast their votes in an election. Never before had the family of a prominent Soviet official been accorded such exposure.

To the Soviet politician, public appeal has not traditionally been a major consideration. But Gorbachev emerged as a public figure who was prepared to play to the crowd. At a Party meeting in Leningrad's historic Smolny Institute in May 1985, his colleagues were quick to note that, by speaking on an impromptu basis, the new leader was able to impart to his address an immediacy — betokening true concern — that would never have been communicated had he merely read from notes. Calling for an end to waste and laziness, and stressing that everyone would be required to work as hard as possible, Gorbachev declared: "Those who do not in-

A guerrilla of the Nicaraguan Democratic Front (FDN) — a U.S.-backed organization opposing Nicaragua's left-wing government — stands guard in a Nicaraguan village in August 1983. The fact that the USSR is providing assistance to the Nicaraguan government continues to cause much friction between the Soviet government and the Reagan administration.

UPI/BETTMANN NEWSPHOTOS

tend to adjust and who are an obstacle to solving these tasks must simply get out of the way. Get out of the way! Don't be a hindrance!"

In his speeches, Gorbachev employed forceful, pragmatic language in a manner that put his message across extremely effectively. His bold, earthy style was reminiscent of Khrushchev's. Gorbachev, however, did not resort to the kind of undignified bluster that often characterized Khrushchev's more impassioned performances. A certain aloofness has generally been expected of Soviet politicians, and Gorbachev seemed to be adept at maintaining this aloofness even when speaking bluntly and directly.

For all his preoccupation with domestic politics and the domestic economy, Gorbachev was forced to take an active interest in foreign affairs during his first year in office. The war in Afghanistan was bogged down in bloody stalemate, and tensions were still severe in the Middle East. Relations with Western Europe and the United States were somewhere between distant and cool, largely due to Soviet unhappiness with the U.S. government's ongoing rearmament program. The Soviets were particularly concerned about the Reagan administration's decision to proceed with research and development for the Strategic Defense Initiative project — an enormously complex and technologically advanced system of ground- and space-based defenses against nuclear missiles. The Soviet leadership recognized that any attempt by the Soviet Union to build a similar system of its own would entail a massive diversion of money, manpower, technology, and research facilities from the civilian sector to the military, devastating the country's consumer economy and causing living standards to plummet as financing for essential services declined.

Gorbachev was determined to break the deadlock in U.S.-Soviet relations and recognized that direct negotiations would be essential to achieving a rapprochement. Since Soviet diplomacy has traditionally first tested shallow waters before taking a major plunge, it was announced that Gorbachev would first pay an official visit to France and meet with Reagan later. France was, from Moscow's point of view, a logical choice. Although France is allied politically with NATO, it maintains an independent military policy and is something of a maverick in the international arena, intent on pursuing its own vision of grandeur. Another consideration influencing the Soviet decision was the fact that France and the Soviet Union had enjoyed exceptionally good relations during the detente years of the 1970s.

Early in October 1985, Gorbachev and his wife Raisa arrived in Paris. As they had been in London, they were accorded celebrity status by the media. In London, Gorbachev had been merely a high-ranking Kremlin official; now, as general secretary of the CPSU, he was the most important man in the Soviet

Instead of wasting the next 10 to 15 years by developing new weapons in space, allegedly designed to make nuclear arms useless, would it not be more sensible to eliminate those arms?
—MIKHAIL GORBACHEV responding to U.S. President Reagan's Strategic Defense Initiative proposal

Gorbachev and U.S. President Ronald Reagan attend the ceremony marking the conclusion of their summit meeting in Geneva, November 21, 1985. Among the topics discussed by the two leaders were arms control, the Strategic Defense Initiative, human rights, and the Soviet occupation of Afghanistan.

UPI/BETTMANN NEWSPHOTOS

Troops of the U.S.-backed National Union for the Total Independence of Angola (UNITA) — a right-wing political and military organization that is seeking to overthrow Angola's Soviet-backed ruling party, the Popular Front for the Liberation of Angola (MPLA) — parade in Jamba, Angola, in May 1984. The Soviet presence in Angola has been defended by Gorbachev as justifiable assistance to "people who are conducting a national war of liberation."

hierarchy. Gorbachev did not seem remotely fazed by his new responsibilities, even when he found himself confronted by the elitist splendors of French diplomatic protocol. From the very outset of Gorbachev's visit to France, it became apparent to Western observers that Gorbachev was not the kind of politician who uses his public-relations abilities to smother his audiences with mere platitudes. Gorbachev's remarks had content. In a speech to the French parliament, he declared: "We [the Soviet government] are fully conscious of the weaknesses in our work and of the difficulties and problems which are often quite serious enough." He stressed that the Soviet government placed great importance on international harmony, and suggested that the division of the world into communist and noncommunist camps need not be an obstacle to such harmony. On the eve of his visit to France, he had appeared on French television, informing viewers that: "We all live in one house . . . even though some enter this house through one entrance and others through another entrance. We must cooperate within this house." As Soviet citizens watching scenes from the visit on television were quick to observe, Gorbachev had about him a new air of certainty and decisiveness.

Gorbachev's self-assurance was particularly evident during a televised press conference held at the end of the visit. Gorbachev and French President François Mitterrand appeared together to answer journalists' questions. To some questions, Gorbachev gave detailed answers; others, he turned aside with a joke and a smile. But on hearing questions concerning such subjects as political prisoners in the Soviet Union, the Soviet government's drastic cutbacks in the number of exit visas granted to Soviet Jews who wished to leave the country, and the British government's recent expulsion of Soviet diplomats accused of spying, Gorbachev displayed impatience, even anger, at what he considered impertinences. In general, however, Gorbachev struck a conciliatory pose, emphasizing the need for the United States and the Soviet Union to reach agreement on how best to preserve world peace. "We have gotten to the point," he said, "where it is not enough to say, yes, we are in favor of a better world, while not being willing to go ahead with practical steps."

Gorbachev's colleagues regarded the visit to France as a major diplomatic success. The general secretary had secured the Soviet view of world affairs substantial exposure in the Western media. The Soviet hierarchy's satisfaction was very much in evidence when Gorbachev was greeted by his colleagues at Moscow's Sheremetyevo airport. Such receptions are usually governed by very strict protocol: the reception committee, tailored to the prominence of the returning traveler, offers stern handshakes and polite comments. On this occasion, however, Gorbachev and his entourage descended from the plane to be met by Gromyko and the other Politburo members, who crowded enthusiastically around Gorbachev, obviously delighted by their leader's performance in Paris.

Six weeks later, Gorbachev went abroad again, this time to Geneva for a summit meeting with Reagan — the first face-to-face encounter between an American leader and a Soviet leader since Brezhnev's time.

The two protagonists and their advisers hoped very much that the negotiations would be productive. Both Reagan and Gorbachev had had plenty of time to prepare for the meeting. Their aides, however, were understandably nervous about how the two men would get along. Reagan was, and had been for many years, an ardent and outspoken anticommunist, and he often attacked Soviet policy in harsh and uncompromising terms. Gorbachev, as had been demonstrated in Paris, had little patience with foreign criticism of Soviet internal affairs. Even whether Nancy Reagan and Raisa Gorbachev would find each other's company pleasant was a matter of constant debate. When the talks began, however, it became apparent that both leaders were anxious to have the meeting succeed.

The first private meeting between Reagan and Gorbachev was held on November 19, 1985, and was hosted by the American delegation, which was based in the Villa Fleur d'Eau, a beautiful chateau

> *He doesn't like them, and he doesn't trust them. But over the last four years, he's come to understand that it's important to have some sort of relationship with them.*
> —U.S. foreign policy counselor, on President Reagan's attitude towards Soviet leaders

Former Soviet diplomat and UN Undersecretary General Arkady Shevchenko, the highest-ranking official ever to defect to the United States, talks to reporters in July 1985. The defection to the West of not only government officials but also major writers, dancers, and musicians dissatisfied with the lack of artistic freedom in the USSR is a continuing source of embarrassment to the Soviets.

on the shores of Lake Geneva. Although the meeting had been scheduled to take only 15 minutes, it ended up lasting just over an hour. The main themes of this first discussion were the mutual distrust that had come to characterize relations between the United States and the Soviet Union and the regional rivalries between the two countries. Reagan criticized the Soviet government for sending Soviet advisers to Nicaragua (where U.S.-backed right-wing forces were seeking to overthrow a democratically elected left-wing government), and also stated that, in his opinion, the Soviets had no right to be in Afghanistan. "This is Soviet aggression," he declared. "It is a destabilizing act." Gorbachev replied by insisting that the people whom the Soviets were aiding were "conducting a national war of liberation."

The talks that took place on the afternoon of the same day concentrated on the Americans' SDI project. Conversation became extremely heated at times, and no agreement was reached. Gorbachev declared, "It looks as though we have arrived at a dead end." Reagan then suggested continuing the

The appointment of Nikolai Ryzhkov (front row, left) to the office of prime minister of the Soviet Union is ratified by vote on November 25, 1985. A staunch supporter of Gorbachev's program for the revitalization of the Soviet economy, Ryzhkov was formerly first deputy chairman of Gosplan (the State Planning Commission).

discussion in a more congenial atmosphere, and the two men, accompanied only by their interpreters, walked down to a small cottage close to the shores of the lake. There, Reagan produced from his pocket a proposal, written in Russian, calling for a 50 percent cut in both sides' nuclear weapons. It did not call for eliminating SDI, however, and Gorbachev dismissed it. "We just disagree," he is reported to have said. After some further discussion, Reagan and Gorbachev walked back up through the grounds of the Villa Fleur d'Eau, still talking so animatedly that their interpreters had a hard time keeping up. It was at this point that Reagan suggested another summit, and they both invited each other to visit their respective capitals.

Altogether, Gorbachev and Reagan had six private meetings, spending more than five hours together. They had candid discussions about the SDI project, Jewish emigration from the USSR, and several other issues.

Occasionally, the discussions grew testy; but decorum was maintained even when the talks became, in Gorbachev's own words, "extremely sharp." The joint statement released at the end of the summit glossed over the fact that no agreements had been reached, but emphasized that a certain rapport had been established. "The president and I have done a huge amount of work," said Gorbachev. "We've packed a lot into the last two days," added Reagan.

With the exception of the Geneva negotiations, Gorbachev's dialogue with the United States largely consisted of a stream of public policy statements made directly to the press. White House officials complained that, by keeping the exchange public and bypassing the normal diplomatic channels, Gorbachev was actually creating the impasse in bilateral relations that he so often declared himself eager to break. Starting with his Easter 1985 announcement of a six-month freeze on the deployment of Soviet medium-range missiles in Eastern Europe and the western Soviet Union, Gorbachev announced a number of similarly well-publicized policy initiatives, including further offers on missile reductions. Some Western commentators began to

Gorbachev meets with Libyan head of state Muammar al-Qaddafi in Moscow on October 10, 1985. Soviet support for Qaddafi, who has gained worldwide notoriety as an alleged sponsor of Arab terrorism, is a major cause of friction between the USSR and the West.

feel that the "Gorbachev glamour" was fading, however, and that the Gorbachev renowned for his grin was pursuing much the same foreign policy goals as his stony-faced predecessors.

Further evidence that Gorbachev did not intend radically to change the Soviet system, and that he had less room to maneuver within the system than sympathetic Western commentators would like to imagine, was provided by Gorbachev's speech to the Twenty-Seventh Congress of the CPSU, which took place in Moscow in February 1986.

It is at the Party congresses that the general secretary of the CPSU presents the policies that will govern all Party activities for the next five years. Prior to the Twenty-Seventh Congress, hopes had been high that sweeping reforms would be announced. A major factor reinforcing people's hopes had been that Gorbachev was scheduled to give his key address on February 25, 1986 — 30 years to the day after Khrushchev, speaking at the Twentieth Congress of the CPSU, had delivered his speech denouncing Stalin and the excesses that had been perpetrated against the Party and the people on the dictator's orders.

In his address, which lasted five and a half hours, Gorbachev made official the reforms he already initiated. The fundamental structures of the Soviet economy were to be left intact. The only departure from tradition was Gorbachev's occasional humor and spontaneity. Once, when he lost his place, the general secretary looked up from his notes, smiled sheepishly, and said, "Excuse me, comrades, I seemed to have skipped the passages on Lenin's principal thoughts." This quip provoked appreciative, but somewhat nervous, laughter from an audience accustomed to hearing the works of Lenin referred to in terms as reverential as those used by devout Christians concerning the Bible. Gorbachev's joke at the expense of the long-established practice of quoting Lenin as the ultimate authority on all matters relating to the Soviet state was, perhaps, the most daring element of his presentation.

The details of Gorbachev's program proved far more predictable than his performance. The general

It is so simplistic. Good Guy Mikhail offers to get rid of all nuclear missiles while Ron the Hawk lumbers on with his antimissile system. It is going to be a difficult task to explain to public opinion that in the real world it is the small print that really matters, not the grandiose initiatives.

—British diplomat, on Gorbachev's nuclear disarmament proposal secretary did criticize the inertia of the Brezhnev years, but he focused on the future, not the past. As he had in many of his previous speeches, he emphasized the importance of "intensifying" the economy — making industry and agriculture more modern and efficient on a strictly socialist basis. There would be no wholesale transition to a market economy. However, more decisions would be made by factory and farm managers, and incentive schemes for workers and managers would be introduced. Gorbachev also called for changes in pricing policy. Prices would no longer be fixed by central state agencies; they would, instead, reflect factors such as product quality and consumer demand.

With reference to international issues, Gorbachev denounced terrorism, expressed willingness to withdraw Soviet forces from Afghanistan once that country's internal political situation had been stabilized, and declared that peaceful coexistence with the West was the only rational course for the future. On a less conciliatory note, he condemned the Reagan administration's approach to arms control as unconstructive and evidence of bad faith, and again denounced America's plans for the militarization of space.

There were no major surprises in Gorbachev's address, and none should have been expected. Gorbachev had always shown himself to be a patient, practical Party official, carefully laying the groundwork before taking action. Since he could well be in power for another 20 or 25 years, he could afford to be patient. Bureaucracies everywhere have always resisted change, and the Soviet establishment is no exception. Gorbachev's low-key approach, combining persistent pressure with a keen appreciation of when to compromise, could well prove a much more effective way of improving the system than a dramatic overhaul — which might provoke serious resistance from the diehard conservatives in the Soviet establishment — could ever be.

From a 1986 perspective, what observations can be made about Mikhail Gorbachev? Unlike American presidents, Gorbachev faces no constitutional limit

AP/WIDE WORLD PHOTOS

Behind bars, in a symbolic gesture of unity, Avital Shcharansky demands the release of her husband, Anatoly, in September 1985. An outspoken critic of the Soviet government, Shcharansky had been sent to a prison camp in 1978. By February 1986 the pressure of world opinion forced the Soviets to free Shcharansky, who then joined his wife in Israel.

Internationally renowned Russian concert pianist Vladimir Horowitz — who so loathed the policies of his country's communist rulers that he abandoned his homeland in 1924 and swore that he would never return — plays at the Moscow Conservatory on April 18, 1986. Horowitz's decision to visit the land of his birth for the first time in 62 years surprised both his friends and the Soviet government.

Now is a wonderful time. Everything that yesterday was said at the family table or in smoking rooms or in narrow circles is now being said openly.

—*Izvestia*
Soviet newspaper, commenting on the Gorbachev regime

on his tenure. Many Soviet citizens expect that Gorbachev will still be general secretary in the year 2000 if his health remains as robust as it is at present. What does that mean for the Soviet Union? Innumerable factors can make a mockery of even the best-informed predictions, but, based on Gorbachev's background, both personal and political, and upon his actions since he became leader, it is possible at least to begin to answer that question.

On the economic front, Gorbachev and the intelligent, ambitious men he has gathered around him will strive to increase industrial and agricultural production, both by improving worker discipline and by providing greater incentives. On the political front, they will endeavor to maintain the status quo and to enhance the Party's credibility with the people. The Party — perhaps a more efficient and less self-serving Party — will continue to enjoy the supremacy it has possessed since 1917. Dissent will not be tolerated: Marxism-Leninism will remain the guiding philosophy of the CPSU. On the diplomatic front, Gorbachev and his colleagues will do everything within their power to dissuade present and future U.S. governments from continuing with the SDI project — the Soviet domestic program cannot be achieved otherwise. Should they fail in that particular endeavor, the Party will almost certainly capitulate to the Soviet military's demands that the threat posed by SDI be neutralized — either by building hundreds more missiles or by constructing a similar system. Also on the diplomatic front, the Soviets will continue to press for advantage wherever possible — in Central America, Africa, and the Middle East.

Gorbachev seems to be comfortably in command, but it is probably too soon to assume that he has all the opposition safely under control. The Soviet military may prove to be the most serious threat to his — and the Party's — authority. If he is to remain in command, and realize his vision for the Soviet Union, he must retain the respect of the majority of his peers and constituents. But for now, the man in charge in the Soviet Union is Mikhail Sergeevich Gorbachev, the man from Stavropol.

Gorbachev and his colleagues at the commencement of the Twenty-Seventh Congress of the CPSU, February 25, 1986. During his opening speech to the congress, Gorbachev declared: "The Soviet Union is determined to justify the hopes of the people of our two countries and of the whole world who are expecting concrete steps, practical actions, and tangible agreements from the leaders of the USSR and the USA on how to curb the arms race."

Further Reading

Butson, Thomas G. *Gorbachev: A Biography.* Briarcliff Manor, N.Y.: Stein and Day, 1985.

Dornberg, John. *Brezhnev: The Masks of Power.* New York: Basic Books, 1974.

Ebon, Martin. *The Andropov File.* New York: McGraw-Hill Book Company, 1983.

Frankland, Mark. *Khrushchev.* New York: Stein and Day, 1967.

Goldman, Marshall I. *U.S.S.R. in Crisis: The Failure of an Economic System.* New York: W.W. Norton & Co., 1983.

Medvedev, Zhores A. *Andropov.* New York: W.W. Norton & Co., 1983.

———. *Gorbachev.* New York: W.W. Norton & Co., 1986.

Shipler, David. *Russia: Broken Idols, Solemn Dreams.* New York: Times Books, 1983.

Steele, Jonathan, and Eric Abraham. *Andropov in Power.* Garden City, N.Y.: Doubleday and Co., Inc., 1984.

Chronology

March 2, 1931	Born Mikhail Sergeevich Gorbachev in Privolnoye near Stavropol, USSR
1941	Adolf Hitler breaks his World War II nonaggression pact with Stalin; Germany invades the Soviet Union
1950–55	Gorbachev studies law at Moscow State University
1952	Joins the Komsomol (Young Communist League)
1954	Elected head of the Komsomol at Moscow State University
1955	Returns to Stavropol and works as a minor Komsomol official
1958	Named first secretary of the Stavropol regional Komsomol
1963	Becomes chief of the agricultural department for the Stavropol region
1966	Named first secretary of the Stavropol city Communist party organization
1967	Completes a correspondence course at the Stavropol Agricultural Institute, graduating with a degree in agronomy
1970	Named first secretary of the regional party committee
1971	Becomes a member of the Central Committee of the Communist party of the Soviet Union
Nov. 1978	Becomes Central Committee agricultural secretary
Nov. 17, 1979	Promoted to candidate membership in the Politburo
Dec. 1979	Soviet troops depose President Amin of Afghanistan and install a pro-Soviet government
Oct. 1980	Gorbachev promoted to full membership in the Politburo
1981	Soviets step in to reorganize the Polish government and encourage the imposition of martial law to quell growing dissent in Poland
Nov. 1982	Gorbachev's mentor, Yuri Andropov, becomes the leader of the Soviet Union
Sept. 1, 1983	Korean Airlines flight originating in the United States is shot down while flying over Soviet territory
Feb. 1984	Andropov dies; Konstantin Chernenko becomes the Soviet leader
Dec. 1984	Gorbachev visits Great Britain and meets with Prime Minister Margaret Thatcher
March 1985	Chernenko dies; Gorbachev becomes general secretary of the Communist party's Central Committee and leader of the Soviet Union
Oct. 1985	Meets with French President Mitterrand in Paris
Nov. 1985	Summit meeting with American President Reagan in Geneva, Switzerland, to discuss U.S.-Soviet relations and the nuclear arms race

Index

Thomas Butson has been assistant news editor of the *New York Times* since 1968. He is also the author of *Pierre Trudeau* in the Chelsea House series WORLD LEADERS PAST & PRESENT.

Arthur M. Schlesinger, jr., taught history at Harvard for many years and is currently Albert Schweitzer Professor of the Humanities at City University of New York. He is the author of numerous highly praised works in American history and has twice been awarded the Pulitzer Prize. He served in the White House as special assistant to Presidents Kennedy and Johnson.